The American Dream in the 21st Century

The American Dream
IN THE 21st Century

EDITED BY

Sandra L. Hanson
John Kenneth White

TEMPLE UNIVERSITY PRESS
Philadelphia

TEMPLE UNIVERSITY PRESS
Philadelphia, Pennsylvania 19122
www.temple.edu/tempress

Library of Congress Cataloging-in-Publication Data

The American dream in the 21st century / edited by Sandra L. Hanson
and John Kenneth White.
     p.   cm.
Includes bibliographical references and index.
ISBN 978-1-4399-0314-8 (cloth : alk. paper)
ISBN 978-1-4399-0315-5 (pbk. : alk. paper)
ISBN 978-1-4399-0316-2 (e-book)
     1. United States—Social conditions—21st century.   2. United States—
Economic conditions—21st century.   3. United States—Civilization—
21st century.   4. Nationalism—United States.   5. Social values—
United States.   I. Hanson, Sandra L.   II. White, John Kenneth, 1952–

HN59.2.A448 2011
306.0973'0905—dc22   2010050110

⊗ The paper used in this publication meets the requirements of the
American National Standard for Information Sciences—Permanence
of Paper for Printed Library Materials, ANSI Z39.48-1992

Printed in the United States of America

2 4 6 8 9 7 5 3 1

To my brothers, Jeff, Steve, and Jim,
who shared in the American Dream with me.
—SLH

To my sister, Janet Raymond,
who also shared in the American Dream with me.
—JKW

To our late colleague Dean Hoge
and the Life Cycle Institute community.
—SLH and JKW

Contents

The Making and Persistence of the American Dream

John Kenneth White
Sandra L. Hanson

HE AMERICAN DREAM remains a vibrant concept that Americans comprehend and define in various ways as relevant to their own life experiences. The endurance of this "great epic," as it was once so famously described (Adams 1941, 405), is remarkable, especially given the depressions, recessions, economic contractions, and battles over civil rights, women's rights, and gender equality that the United States has witnessed over the years. These economic struggles have been hard and are presently ongoing, starting with the severe economic downturn that began in December 2007 and resulted in government bailouts of the U.S. banking and automotive industries and the election of Barack Obama to the presidency, all before the end of a single calendar year. But other struggles, too, have caused citizens to redefine the American Dream. For much of our history, African Americans and women were excluded from its promise. It would be left to Martin Luther King and feminist leaders to enlarge the American Dream to include themselves and to encourage their constituencies to have a stake in its success. In 2008, Americans voted in their first African American president. This dramatic moment in American history combined with one of the most severe economic downturns since the Great Depression provide the backdrop for this volume on the American Dream.

The American Dream throughout History

The resiliency of the American Dream can be traced to the Declaration of Independence in 1776 and its promise that citizens of the new nation were already endowed by their Creator with certain inalienable rights, including life and liberty, and that these same people were entitled to engage in many varied pursuits of happiness. These pursuits of happiness often ended with many finding some degree of fulfillment. Writing in 1831, Alexis de Tocqueville declared that the Americans he encountered had "acquired or retained sufficient education and fortune to satisfy their own wants." Tocqueville added that they "owe nothing to any man, they expect nothing from any man, they acquire the habit of always considering themselves as standing alone, and *they are apt to imagine that their whole destiny is in their own hands*" (Tocqueville 1989, 194; emphasis added).

These sentiments give the American Dream its staying power. Not surprisingly, Americans have looked to their leaders since the nation's founding to reaffirm the promise of the American Dream, with its guarantees of fuller liberties and a better life for all. In his 2009 inaugural address, Obama gave testimony to the Dream's endurance, citing his own life's journey to become the first African American president: "This is the meaning of our liberty and creed, why men and women and children of every race and every faith can join in celebration across this magnificent mall. And why a man whose father less than sixty years ago might not have been served at a local restaurant can now stand before you to take a most sacred oath" (Obama 2009).

Yet it is not only in government documents or presidential speeches that the American Dream finds expression. The popular culture also has given the American Dream a powerful voice. Contrasting his gritty childhood in Brooklyn at the turn of the twentieth century with his stunning success on Broadway by the age of twenty-five, playwright Moss Hart concluded that the American Dream belonged not only to him but to everyone: "It was possible in this wonderful city for that nameless little boy—for any of its millions—to have a decent chance to scale the walls and achieve what they wished. Wealth, rank, or an imposing name counted for nothing. The only credential the city asked was the boldness to dream. For those who did, it unlocked its gates and its treasures, not caring who they were or where they came from" (Hart 1959, 436). Years later, the Brian De Palma film *Scarface* had a trailer describing the main character this way: "He loved the American Dream. With a vengeance" (Kamp 2009).

Surprisingly, the term "American Dream" is of relatively recent vintage. Journalist Walter Lippmann first used the term "American Dream" in a 1914 book titled *Drift and Mastery* in which he urged readers to find a new Dream for the twentieth century that would end the malaise of government inaction that had allowed American politics to aimlessly drift (Jillson 2004, 6). But historian James Truslow Adams popularized the phrase "American Dream" in 1931. In his book titled *The Epic of America* (and whose working title was *The American Dream*), Adams described the American Dream in terms Hart would recognize: "that dream of a land in which life should be better and richer and fuller for every man, with opportunity for each according to ability or achievement" (Adams 1941, 404). But, for Adams, the American Dream involved something more than mere acquisition of wealth and fame:

> It is not a dream of motor cars and high wages merely, but a dream of social order in which each man and each woman shall be able to attain to the fullest stature of which they are innately capable, and be recognized by others for what they are, regardless of the fortuitous circumstances of their birth. . . . It has been a dream of being able to grow to fullest development as man and woman, unhampered by the barriers which had slowly been erected in older civilizations, unrepressed by social orders which had developed for the benefit of classes rather than for the simple human being of any and every class. And that dream has been realized more fully in actual life here than anywhere else, though very imperfectly even among ourselves. (Ibid., 404–405)

At its core, the American Dream represents a state of mind—that is, an enduring optimism given to a people who might be tempted to succumb to the travails of adversity, but who, instead, repeatedly rise from the ashes to continue to build a great nation. Even in the midst of the Great Depression, Adams was confident that the United States would overcome its difficulties and that the American Dream would endure thanks to a prevailing optimism that sustains it. This die-hard optimism, Adams declared, had already carried the nation from its primitive beginnings into the twentieth century and remained the source of its continued successes:

> Beginning with a guard scarce sufficient to defend the stockade at Jamestown against a few naked Indians, we grew until we were able to select from nearly 25,000,000 men of military age such

millions as we would to hurl back at our enemies across the sea, only nine generations later. A continent which scarce sufficed to maintain a half million savages now supports nearly two hundred and fifty times that number of as active and industrious people as there are in the world. The huge and empty land has been filled with homes, roads, railways, schools, colleges, hospitals, and all the comforts of the most advanced material civilization. (Ibid., 401–402)

Notably, Adams penned these words at a time when economic fear was rampant, the stock market had collapsed two years before, the ineffectual Herbert Hoover was president, and the nation's very survival seemed very much in doubt. By 1933, the stock market had lost 75 percent of its 1929 value, national income had been cut in half, exports were at their lowest levels since 1904, and more than six hundred thousand properties (mostly farms) had been foreclosed (Alter 2006, 148). Surveying the economic desolation in January 1933, former president Calvin Coolidge remarked: "In other periods of depression it has always been possible to see some things which were solid and upon which you could base hope. But as I look about me I see nothing to give ground for such hope—nothing of man" (Ibid.). (Within days, Coolidge was dead.) Although Franklin D. Roosevelt's New Deal brought economic relief, the new president knew that to make his efforts long-lasting, they should be linked to a new American Dream. Accordingly, Roosevelt told his fellow Democrats upon accepting renomination in 1936: "Liberty requires opportunity to make a living decent according to the standard of the time, a living that gives man not only enough to live by, but something to live for." Without the opportunity to make a living, Roosevelt continued, "life was no longer free; liberty no longer real; men could no longer follow the pursuit of happiness" (Roosevelt 1936).

Yet even in the midst of a Great Depression, Americans sensed that their collective futures would be bright, if not for themselves, then surely for their heirs. A poll the Roper Organization conducted in 1938 found only 30 percent agreed that a top limit should be imposed on incomes, with anyone exceeding that limit remitting the excess to the federal government in the form of excise taxes; 61 percent *disagreed* (Roper Organization, 1938). Americans believed economic prosperity was possible and achieving it would ratify the American Dream whose promise of hard work (not good luck) is the path to prosperity. Indeed, through every period of triumph and tragedy, Adams maintained that the American Dream was the glue that kept the country together: "We have a long and arduous road to travel if we are to realize the American Dream in the life of our nation, but if we fail, there is nothing left but the eternal round. The alternative is the failure of self-government, the failure of the common man to rise to full stature, the failure of all that the American Dream has held of hope and promise for mankind" (Adams 1941, 416).

Adams's words have echoed throughout the decades, particularly at the onset of Obama's presidency. Like Roosevelt before him, Obama has had to summon the nation from the sloughs of despair. Accepting the Democratic presidential nomination in 2008, Obama sought to cast himself as an exemplar of the American Dream and the best person who could revive and reclaim it for the rest of us:

> Four years ago, I stood before you and told you my story, of the brief union between a young man from Kenya and a young woman from Kansas who weren't well-off or well-known, but shared a belief that in America their son could achieve whatever he put his mind to.
>
> It is that promise that's always set this country apart, that through hard work and sacrifice each of us can pursue our individual dreams, but still come together as one American family, to ensure that the next generation can pursue their dreams, as well. That's why I stand here tonight. Because for 232 years, at each moment when that promise was in jeopardy, ordinary men and women, students and soldiers, farmers and teachers, nurses and janitors, found the courage to keep it alive.
>
> We meet at one of those defining moments, a moment when our nation is at war, our economy is in turmoil, and the American promise has been threatened once more. (Obama 2008)

The threat of which Obama spoke was very real. Even as he uttered these words, the nation was mired in a recession judged by most economists to have been the worst since the Great Depression of the 1930s. More than 7,200,000 jobs were lost; the official unemployment rate exceeded 10 percent for the first time in twenty-nine years; and the number of Americans who gave up looking for work or were marginally attached workers hit the 17 percent mark (Fox 2009). Taking note of these dismal statistics, Obama declared that they represented "the American Dream [going] in reverse" (Kamp 2009).

Despite these adverse statistics and continued uncertainty regarding whether the prescriptions the Obama administration has issued for economic revival will work, faith in the American Dream itself remains strong. In 2009, 75 percent told pollsters from CBS News and the *New York Times* that they had either already achieved the American Dream or that they expected to achieve it; only one in five said it was unattainable (CBS News/*New York Times* 2009). Sociologist Barry Glassner explained why the American Dream was not imperiled, despite the straightened economic circumstances:

> You want to hold onto your dream when times are hard. For the vast majority of Americans at every point in history, the prospect of achieving the American Dream has been slim, but the promise has been huge. . . . At its core, this notion that anyone can be president, or anyone can be a billionaire, is absurd. A lot of Americans work hard, but they don't become president and they don't become billionaires. (Seelye 2009)

Yet for many Americans, holding onto the American Dream has become increasingly more difficult. During his presidency, Bill Clinton defined the American Dream this way: "If you work hard and play by the rules, you should be given a chance to go as far as your God-given ability will take you" (Jillson 2004, 7). But in the years since, many Americans have hit a glass ceiling. In 2002, Barbara Ehrenreich began to hear from college graduates and white-collar workers who upbraided her for not taking note of their hard-luck stories, "despite doing everything else right." As one unhappy middle-class correspondent told Ehrenreich:

> Try investigating people like me who didn't have babies in high school, who made good grades, who work hard and don't kiss a lot of ass and instead of getting promoted or paid fairly must regress to working for $7/hr., having their student loans in perpetual deferment, living at home with their parents, and generally exist in debt which they feel they may never get out of. (Ehrenreich 2005, 1–2)

As Phyllis Moen and Patricia Roehling have observed, "The American Dream is itself a metaphor for occupational success, a metaphor that works for the winners of the educational and occupational career game, but that remains elusive for growing numbers of men and women across age, class, educational, racial, ethnic, and geographical divides" (Moen and Roehling 2005, 188).

Even so, the American Dream still endures, and that endurance is a testament to its power. Some years ago, singer/songwriter Bruce Springsteen wondered aloud in a song entitled "The River" whether the American Dream was a lie or it represented something worse (White 1990, 28). But this is a question that most Americans do not want to consider. Instead of questioning the American Dream, Americans are more likely to blame themselves when things do not turn out as they hoped. Nearly a half century ago, a mechanic admitted as much in an interview:

> I could have been a lot better off but through my own foolishness, I'm not. What causes poverty? Foolishness. When I came out of the service, my wife had saved a few dollars and I had a few bucks. I wanted to have a good time, I'm throwing money away like water. Believe me, had I used my head right, I could have had a house. I don't feel sorry for myself, what happened, happened, you know. Of course you pay for it. (Lane 1962, 69)

Years later, an Iowa farmer facing foreclosure expressed a similar view: "My boys all made good. It's their old man who failed" (Malcolm 1987).

The fact is that the American Dream is deeply embedded in American mythology and in the consciousness of its citizens. That is exactly what gives the American Dream its staying power, even in times when it seems as though it should surely die. After all, myths last because they are dreams fulfilled in our imaginations. So it is with the American Dream. And because it finds fulfillment either in one's own life or in the lives of others, Americans are ever more devoted to it. In 1978, Garry Wills famously observed that in the United States, one must adopt the American Dream "wholeheartedly, proclaim it, prove one's devotion to it" (Wills 1978, xxii). Twenty years later, political scientist Alan Wolfe interviewed Henry Johnson, a successful, middle-class black man from DeKalb County, Georgia, who declared his ongoing faith in the American Dream despite the adversities he had encountered in life: "I think the American Dream is alive and well, and I think I could sell the American Dream to my kids through myself. This stuff about working hard and being morally sound and the more you give, the more you receive and things will come to you. I think those are all things that are not fantasies. Those things can happen and, through my own experiences, those things have happened. . . . Like I said, I believe in the American Dream, I do." Sitting nearby, Johnson's wife told the interviewer, "Wow, that was good; quote him on that" (Wolfe 1998, 317–318).

One reason the American Dream endures is that it has been closely intertwined with deeply held American values, especially freedom and equality of opportunity. In a 2008 poll, 75 percent strongly agreed with this statement: "America is unique among all nations, because it is founded on the ideals of freedom, equality, and opportunity" (Greenberg Quinlan Rosner Research 2008). Pollsters for CBS News and the *New York Times* found 27 percent of respondents specifically linked the American Dream to the values of freedom and equality of opportunity. Typical among the responses were these:

"Freedom to live our own life."
"Someone could start from nothing."
"That everybody has a fair chance to succeed."
"To become whatever I want to be."
"To be healthy and have nice family and friends."
"More like Huck Finn; escape to the unknown; follow your
    dreams." (Seelye 2009)

The linking of the American Dream to equality of opportunity is particularly important to understanding the Dream's endurance. Equality of opportunity is a powerful concept, because, unlike other individual rights that can be easily taken away by authoritarian governments (e.g., freedoms of speech and religious worship), it is a state of mind that is virtually impossible to eliminate. As the historian Adams wrote, "I once had an intelligent young Frenchman as a guest in New York, and after a few days I asked him what struck him most among his new impressions. Without hesitation, he replied, 'The way that everyone of every sort looks you right in the eye, without a thought of inequality'" (Adams 1941, 404). Tocqueville once declared that if given the choice between freedom and equality, most Americans would choose the latter for that very reason (Tocqueville 1989, 96). Although Tocqueville wrote about nineteenth-century Americans, his words still have resonance. Englishman G. K. Chesterton noted that what separated the United States from his native country in the twentieth century was the American commitment to a democratic theory based on the idea of equality: "It is the pure classic conception that no man must aspire to be anything more than a citizen, and that no man should endure anything less." The ideal citizen, said Chesterton, was someone who believed in "an absolute of morals by which all men have a value invariable and indestructible and a dignity as intangible as death" (Chesterton 1922, 16–17). At the onset of the twenty-first century, the words of Adams, Tocqueville, and Chesterton remain Rosetta stones to understanding how the battles over civil rights for African Americans, feminist rights, and gay rights are working their way toward greater equality for more Americans.

As the recent struggles over civil rights, women's rights, and gay rights illustrate, the American Dream is not a static concept. Although Americans have historically associated the American Dream with the values of freedom and equality of opportunity, these values have undergone various iterations over the years. Remarkably, the very first survey concerning the American Dream was not conducted until 1985, when CBS News and the *New York Times* asked a question that explicitly tied the American Dream to the concept of home ownership: "Do you think that people who may never own a house miss out on an important part of the American Dream?" Not surprisingly, 76 percent answered "yes" (CBS News/*New York Times* 1985). Other surveys have demonstrated how powerfully connected the American Dream is to a quantified measure of economic success (particularly educational attainment), including these responses:

84 percent said it meant being able to get a high school education. (*Wall Street Journal* 1986)

79 percent said it meant owning a home. (Penn, Schoen, and Berland Associates 2008)

77 percent said it meant being able to send one's children to college. (Ibid.)

76 percent said it meant being optimistic about the future. (Ibid.)

68 percent said it meant being able to get a college education. (Ibid.)

64 percent said it meant being financially secure enough to have ample time for leisure pursuits. (Ibid.)

61 percent said it meant doing better than your parents did. (Ibid.)

58 percent said it meant being able to start a business on one's own. (Ibid.)

52 percent said it meant being able to rise from clerk or worker to president of a company. (Ibid.)

But although the American Dream remains closely tied to the values of freedom and equality of opportunity, its iterations throughout the years have changed. When a Penn, Schoen, and Berland Associates 2008 study asked respondents to define the American Dream, the responses were more spiritual and vested in emotional, rather than material, security. Substantial majorities considered the following items to be a "major part" of the American Dream:

Having a good family life, 93 percent (Ibid.)

Having quality health care for myself and my family, 90 percent (Ibid.)

Having educational opportunities for myself and my family, 88 percent (Ibid.)

Being able to speak your mind regardless of the positions you take, 85 percent (Ibid.)

Having a comfortable and secure retirement, 85 percent (Ibid.)

Being able to succeed regardless of your family background or where you come from, 82 percent (Ibid.)

Being economically secure and not having to worry about being able to afford things, 81 percent (Ibid.)

Achieving peace in the world, 63 percent (Ibid.)

Having the time to enjoy the good things in life without having to work too many hours, 59 percent (Ibid.)

Reducing the effects of global warming, 56 percent (Ibid.)

Certainly, although economic security continues to define the American Dream, the Dream itself has been broadened to include a greater sense of personal well-being and quality-of-life issues (such as having access to quality health care, working toward world peace, and reducing the harmful effects of global warming).

A Dream in Doubt? No. Harder to Achieve? Yes.

In an early-twentieth-century work titled *Success among the Nations,* historian Emil Reich declared that Americans were possessed "with such an implicit and absolute confidence in their Union and in their future success, that any remark other than laudatory is unacceptable to the majority of them," adding, "We have had many opportunities of hearing public speakers in America cast doubts upon the very existence of God and of Providence, question the historic nature or veracity of the whole fabric of Christianity; but it has never been our fortune to catch the slightest whisper of doubt, the slightest want of faith, in the chief God of America, unlimited belief in the future of America" (Reich 1904, 265–266).

But in recent years, expressions of self-doubt about the nation's future have been uttered more frequently. Vice President Joseph Biden, for one, has said that "the American economic dream has begun to evaporate" (Dionne, Jr. 1987). What is striking is that the vice president made this declaration more than two decades ago as a candidate seeking the Democratic presidential nomination in *1988.* Not surprisingly, when economic difficulties beset the nation, one might suspect (a Great Depression notwithstanding) that the American Dream will take a beating. So it is today. According to the most recent surveys:

75 percent claim the American Dream is not as attainable today as it was when George W. Bush was elected president in 2000. (Zogby International 2008)

59 percent believe the American Dream will be harder for today's children under the age of eighteen to achieve. (Greenberg Quinlan Rosner Research and Public Opinion Strategies 2009)

57 percent say the American Dream will be harder for them to achieve in the next decade. (*Time*/Abt SRBI 2009)

54 percent believe the American Dream has become "impossible" for most people to achieve. (Opinion Research Corporation 2006)

50 percent think they are either "somewhat far" or "very far" from achieving the American Dream. (Henry J. Kaiser Family Foundation/*Washington Post*/Harvard University 2008)

Despite these daunting statistics, faith in the American Dream persists. In March 2009, a moment when the economic crisis was palpable, the Gallup Organization and *USA Today* found an overwhelming 72 percent still agreed with this statement: "If you work hard and play by the rules, you will be able to achieve the American Dream in your lifetime" (Gallup Organization/*USA Today* 2009). Moreover, 69 percent believed their children would achieve the American Dream (Penn, Schoen, and Berland Associates 2008).

In one sense, the American Dream will always remain elusive and, therefore, disappoint us. A 2008 survey makes the point: 84 percent agreed that the American Dream is "a never-ending pursuit [and] I can always do more to achieve it" (Penn, Schoen, and Berland Associates 2008). Achieving the American Dream will always be partly an individual pursuit. Yet it is also a Dream that we entrust to our presidents. The subtitle of Obama's book *The Audacity of Hope* reads "thoughts on reclaiming the American Dream" (Obama 2006). It is not, as Obama suggests, that the American Dream is lost; rather, there is a prevailing sense (and hope) that he can somehow *renew* the American Dream. As Vice President Biden declared in his 1988 presidential quest: "The role of a President in mobilizing our society is to convince all of our citizens that they can and must shape their own future and the nation's future" (Dionne, Jr. 1987). If Obama can fulfill this vital role of the presidency, the American Dream will thrive. If not, the American Dream will still endure, in spite of our disappointments.

The historic economic, political, and social times of this period in the twenty-first century is the context in which we provide an examination of the American Dream. In the pages that follow, experts from multiple disciplines provide insight into the nature and resilience of the American Dream in this time frame, with a special focus on the millennial recession and the election of President Obama. The discussion begins with "Twilight's Gleaming: The American Dream and the Ends of Republics," in which American Studies expert James Cullen provides historical insight into the American Dream by drawing parallels with the Roman republic and empire. Cullen argues that many of the most cherished aspects of the American Dream, such as upward mobility, have clear antecedents in other civilizations. The next two chapters provide a political critique of the American Dream. Historian Michael Kimmage's chapter ("The Politics of the American Dream, 1980 to 2008") examines the Depression, the New Deal, and party platforms to reveal the optimism and enthusiasm for particular versions of the American Dream in the United States. Political scientist John White's chapter on "The Presidency and the Making of the American Dream" also notes historical variation in the Dream in his examination of the American presidency as a place where the American Dream has become personified. Sociologists Jim Loewen and Sandra Hanson provide insight into racial and gender variation in the American Dream in the next two chapters. In his chapter ("Dreaming in Black and White") Loewen examines race-based residential segregation and the Dream of two separate Americas. Hanson ("Whose American Dream? Gender and the American Dream") uses a series of public opinion polls on the American Dream to show how achievement of and attitudes toward the American Dream vary for men and women. American political pollster John Zogby's chapter ("Want Meets Necessity in the New American Dream") compiles decades of public opinion polling data to reveal the nature and strength of the American Dream with a consideration of generational differences, the impact of September 11, the economic downturn, and the Obama presidency. Sociologist William D'Antonio provides a Catholic reflection on the role of religion in defining the Dream and making it achievable for all. In the conclusion ("The American Dream: Where Are We?"), the editors reveal the complexity of the American Dream using sociological, political, and historical frames of reference. They find that although evidence of the Dream's continued existence is abundant, its meaning has been altered and the Great Recession has tempered the Dream itself. This situation remains the case despite the optimism that came with the election of the first African American to the presidency and Obama's repeated attempts to instill public confidence.

Polls

CBS News/*New York Times,* poll, April 1–5, 2009. Text of question: "Do you think you will reach, as you define it, 'The American Dream' in your lifetime, or have you already reached it?" Already reached it, 44 percent; will reach it in my lifetime, 31 percent; will not reach it in my lifetime, 20 percent; don't know/no answer, 5 percent.

CBS News/*New York Times,* poll, January 14–17, 1985. Text of question: "Do you think that people who may never own a house miss out on an important part of the American Dream?" Yes, 76 percent; no, 19 percent; don't know/no answer, 5 percent.

Gallup Organization/*USA Today,* poll, March 2, 2009. Text of question: "Which is closer to your view—if you work hard and play by the rules, you will be able to achieve the American Dream in your lifetime, or even by working hard and playing by the rules, the American Dream is unattainable for you?" If you work hard and play by the rules, you will be able to achieve the American Dream in your lifetime, 72 percent; even by working hard and playing by the rules, the American Dream is unattainable for you, 25 percent; don't know, 2 percent; refused, 1 percent.

Greenberg Quinlan Rosner Research and Public Opinion Strategies, poll, January 27–February 8, 2009. Text of question: "Thinking about young people, do you think it will be easier or harder for them to achieve the American Dream?" Much easier, 13 percent; somewhat easier, 21 percent; somewhat harder, 30 percent; much harder, 29 percent; about the same (volunteered), 3 percent; don't know/refused, 3 percent.

Henry J. Kaiser Family Foundation/*Washington Post*/Harvard University, poll, June 18–July 7, 2008. Text of question: "I'd like to talk to you now about a term with which you are probably familiar: the American Dream. How close are you to achieving the American Dream—are you very close, somewhat close, somewhat far, or very far?" Very close, 8 percent; somewhat close, 35 percent; somewhat far, 27 percent; very far, 23 percent; already achieved it (volunteered), 4 percent; don't know what that is (volunteered), 1 percent; don't know, 2 percent.

Opinion Research Corporation, poll, October 13–15, 2006. Text of question: "Do you agree or disagree: The American Dream has become impossible for most people to achieve?" Agree, 54 percent; disagree, 45 percent; don't know/undecided/refused, 2 percent.

Penn, Schoen, and Berland Associates, poll, June 19–29, 2008. Text of question: "I'm going to read you some possible definitions or descriptions of the American Dream, and for each one I'd like you to tell me if that's very much what you understand the American Dream to mean, or sort of what it means, or not what it means. . . . To own a home." Very much, 79 percent; sort of, 18 percent; not, 3 percent; don't know, 1 percent.

Penn, Schoen, and Berland Associates, poll, June 19–29, 2008. Text of question: "Is it likely your children will achieve the American Dream?" Yes, 69 percent; no, 20 percent; don't know/no answer, 10 percent.

Penn, Schoen, and Berland Associates, poll, June 19–29, 2008. Text of question: "Which is closer to your view? I have set goals for my life that once reached will mean that I have achieved the American Dream. The American Dream is a never-ending pursuit [and] I can always do more to achieve it." I have set goals for my life that once reached will mean that I have achieved the American Dream, 13 percent; the American Dream is a never-ending pursuit [and] I can always do more to achieve it, 84 percent; don't know/no answer, 3 percent.

Roper Organization, poll, November 1938. Text of question: "Do you believe there should be a top limit of income and that anyone getting over that limit should be compelled to turn the excess back to the Government as taxes?" Yes, 30 percent; no, 61 percent; don't know, 9 percent.

Time/Abt SRBI, poll, April 1–5, 2009. Text of question: "People sometimes talk about the American Dream, that is the ability of all Americans to achieve their goals in life through hard work. Would you say that it's going to be easier or harder for Americans to achieve the American Dream in ten years than it is today, or that things won't change much?" Easier, 13 percent; harder, 57 percent; won't change much, 24 percent; no answer/don't know, 5 percent.

Wall Street Journal, poll, October 1986. Text of question: "I'm going to read you some possible definitions or descriptions of the American Dream, and for each one I'd like you to tell me if that's very much what you understand the American Dream to mean, or sort of what it means, or not what it means. . . . To be able to get a high school education." Very much, 84 percent; sort of, 11 percent; not, 4 percent.

Zogby International, poll, May 12–14, 2008. Text of question: "Do you believe that the American Dream is as attainable today as it was eight years ago?" Yes, 24 percent; no, 75 percent; not sure, 2 percent.

References

Adams, J. T. 1941. *The epic of America.* Garden City, NY: Blue Ribbon Books.

Alter, J. 2006. *The defining moment: FDR's hundred days and the triumph of hope.* New York: Simon and Schuster.

Chesterton, G. K. 1922. *What I saw in America.* New York: Dodd, Mead.

Dionne, E. J., Jr. 1987. Biden, offering a 1988 vision, says American Dream is evaporating. *New York Times,* May 15.

Ehrenreich, B. 2005. *Bait and switch.* New York: Metropolitan Books, Henry Holt.

Fox, J. 2009. *Nope, no jobs here.* October 2. Message posted to http://curious capitalist.blogs.time.com/2009/10/02.nope-no-jobs-here.

Hart, M. 1959. *Act one: An autobiography.* New York: Random House.

Jillson, C. 2004. *Pursuing the American Dream: Opportunity and exclusion over four centuries.* Lawrence: University Press of Kansas.

Kamp, D. 2009. Rethinking the American Dream. *Vanity Fair,* April. Available at www.vanityfair.com/culture/features/2009/04/american-dream200904.

Lane, R. 1962. *Political ideology: Why the common man believe what he does.* New York: Free Press.

Malcolm, A. H. 1987. What five families did after losing the farm. *New York Times,* February 4.

Moen, P., and P. Roehling. 2005. *The career mystic: Cracks in the American Dream.* Lanham, MD: Rowman and Littlefield.

Obama, B. 2006. *The audacity of hope: Thoughts on reclaiming the American Dream.* New York: Crown Publishers.

———. 2008. Acceptance speech. Democratic National Convention, Denver, Colorado, August 28.

———. 2009. Inaugural address. Washington, D.C., January 20.

Reich, E. 1904. *Success among the nation.* New York: Harper.

Roosevelt, F. D. 1936. Acceptance speech. Democratic National Convention, Philadelphia, Pennsylvania, June 27. Available at www.2austin.cc.tx.us/1patrick/his2341/fdr36acceptancespeech.htm.

Seelye, K. Q. 2009. What happens to the American Dream in a recession? *New York Times,* May 8.

Tocqueville, A. de. 1989. *Democracy in America.* Vol. II. New York: Alfred A. Knopf.

White, J. K. 1990. *The new politics of old values.* Hanover, NH: University Press of New England.

Wills, G. 1978. *Inventing America.* New York: Vintage Books.

Wolfe, A. 1998. *One nation after all.* New York: Viking.

CHAPTER 1

Twilight's Gleaming

The American Dream and the Ends of Republics

Jim Cullen

> *What is the point of this story?*
> *What information pertains?*
> *The thought that life could be better*
> *Is woven indelibly into our hearts*
> *And our brains*
> —Paul Simon, "Train in the Distance"

COUNT ON A SONGWRITER to capture the essence of an idea more pithily than a scholar ever could. "Train in the Distance," from Paul Simon's overlooked 1983 album, *Hearts and Bones,* is hardly his best-known work. But it is enormously evocative. "Everybody loves the sound of a train in the distance," his narrator sings. "Everybody thinks it's true." The key term in that lyric is "everybody." It is an important one to keep in mind in any discussion of the American Dream. The notion of a better life lies at the core of the Dream. But its resonance rests on a belief that it is widely available—at least for those fortunate enough to live in the United States of America. Everybody dreams, of course, but the great thing about dreaming *here* is that all can feel justified in doing so. What makes the American Dream *American* is not that our Dreams are better than anybody else's; it is the fact that we live in a country constituted of Dreams, whose very justification rests on it being a place where one can, for better or worse, pursue distant goals (Cullen 2003, 182).

Or so I once believed. In recent years, however, I have been thinking a little harder about the word "everybody" and about *whose* hearts and brains are woven indelibly. There was a time I made an argument for a form of American exceptionalism by pointing out that no one speaks of the French Dream or the Chinese Dream. I still think there is some truth to that statement. But I now believe it is not entirely accurate or complete.

One reason why is that in recent years I have begun straying outside my disciplinary pen in American Studies and reading a bit more widely. More specifically, I have become interested in ancient history, particularly that of the Roman republic and empire. This interest was significantly fermented in 2007–2008 by the broadcast of the HBO series *Rome,* which did a marvelous job of evoking the late republic through spectacular sets, exquisite attention to period detail, and wonderful acting. I also read a few novels by Steven Saylor, which feature a fictional character, Gordianus the Finder, who works periodically for the great Roman orator and politician Marcus Tullius Cicero, and a couple novels about Cicero himself by British writer Robert Harris.[1]

Whatever errors of fact or interpretation one might find in these works of popular culture, they, along with the more academically reputable books I have been reading, have helped me see that it is possible to discern what might be termed a "Roman Dream" and to believe that the core ideas embedded in such a locution are no anachronism. Cicero also happens to be one of the featured characters in *Rome,* albeit as a man whose best days are behind him when the series opens but who is nevertheless a pivotal player in Roman politics. This is remarkable in part because the real Cicero was known as a so-called "New Man" who rose to the ultimate office of consul despite lacking the usual aristocratic birth or connections. (Julius Caesar, for his part, came from a lowly aristocratic family but attained power as a populist.) Cicero was a singular figure as a writer, orator, and politician, but he was by no means the only person in Roman history to have experienced such upward mobility. Less spectacularly, but perhaps more importantly, non-Roman soldiers in the later empire who served a full term in the army (twenty to twenty-five years) were granted citizenship, a welfare program in a multicultural empire that mingled social inequality and cultural pluralism in

---

[1] See, for example, *Roman Blood* (New York: Minotaur, 1991) and *Catalina's Riddle* (New York: Minotaur, 1993), both part of Saylor's "Sub Rosa" series. Robert Harris has also written a good Cicero novel, *Imperium: A Novel of Ancient Rome* (New York: Simon and Schuster, 2006), featuring a slave who works for the famed orator. He followed it with an account of the Cataline Conspiracy, *Conspirata* (New York: Simon and Schuster, 2010).

a way any contemporary immigrant would recognize. Like the United States prior to 1865, the Roman republic and empire were societies whose labor systems depended on slavery (the United States has grown addicted to cheap industrial labor in the time since). But although in the United States slavery was the chief obstacle in legitimating the American Dream, slaves in Roman society could achieve significant upward mobility in their lifetimes and arguably achieve their freedom more easily than in the United States.[2]

Nor are examples of such mobility limited to ancient Rome. One can see its outlines in the Confucian civil service in Han China, for example, or in the role of the foreign service in nineteenth-century Great Britain. History is replete with examples of figures who aspired, and achieved, far more than their original circumstances would seem to warrant and who did so not because of some mysterious quirk of fate but because a system of one kind or another was in place to help such individuals realize their ambitions, whether religious, political, or social.

Of course, the devil is in the details. The American Dream is not a unitary concept but rather a complex and multifaceted one. Although the Dream in the abstract might be summarized as a belief that anything is possible in some form if one wants it badly enough, the historical reality is one of a series of discrete, and sometimes competing, Dreams: the Dream of upward mobility, the Dream of home ownership, the Dream of racial justice, and so on.

Moreover, complexities and even contradictions marble these Dreams. For example, many American Dreams are considered Dreams of freedom, but freedom can mean different, even antithetical, things. The Pilgrims and Puritans of the seventeenth century were motivated by a Dream of religious freedom. This Dream they understood to mean not religious tolerance (as it did in New Amsterdam, or Pennsylvania) but rather the right to *not* have to tolerate the wickedness from which they longed to escape. Other Dreams of freedom were more economic: The so-called "adventurers" of colonial Virginia sought instant riches. While the Puritans embraced a work ethic to mark time while waiting for a hoped-for salvation, white Virginians hustled in a quest to get slaves to do their work.

---

[2] On the status and prospects of slaves and soldiers, see Lionel Casson, *Everyday Life in Ancient Rome*, exp. ed. (1975; Baltimore: Johns Hopkins University Press, 1998). For a sustained comparison of the American and Roman situations, see Cullen Murphy, *Are We Rome? The Fall of an Empire and the Fate of America* (Boston: Houghton Mifflin, 2007).

The Founding Fathers, for their part, had a Dream of freedom that was more political than economic or religious. The Declaration of Independence was their charter, the Constitution their blueprint. For the literal and figurative denizens of Hollywood, the Dream of freedom was personal: a sense of effortless grace I have dubbed "the Dream of the Coast" (Cullen 2003, ch. 6). Naturally, these classifications were not always hard and clear, but they nevertheless had literal as well as figurative accents.

In any case, those are just American Dreams of freedom. Others, by contrast, were Dreams of equality. Here again, the Puritans are instructive: For them, freedom from a corrupt England and Holland was a means to the end of a beloved New England community, and if the reality never approached the ideal, Puritan life was marked by a sense of egalitarianism rare in the Old World and the New. Racial injustice has been the source of other Dreams of equality. Civil rights leaders from Frederick Douglass through Martin Luther King, Jr., have cast the American Dream in such terms, in realms that ranged from restrooms to the content of one's character.

The freedom/equality duality aside, the American Dream spins on another axis, and one of particular relevance at the end of this essay: public versus private. One of the most prized aspects of the American Dream is that it is deeply personal: In some important sense, there have been as many American Dreams as there have been Americans, and, thanks to immigration, American identity has been something as much imagined and acquired as it has been inherited, reborn with every new citizen. Yet it is also true that the great appeal of the Dream is its decisively public character: In its most mythically appealing form, American opportunity thrives in sunlight. That is true notwithstanding a powerful counter-narrative, one that extends from the Western to *The Sopranos* and its ilk. (But we shall save discussion of *that* HBO series for another day.)

Actually, bringing up a show about organized crime is not coincidental, for it points toward a key question: What role does playing by a set of rules, also known as governance, play in fostering and sustaining the American Dream?

The answer is surprisingly ambiguous. The Declaration of Independence has long functioned as the banner of the American Dream, one repeatedly waved by such figures as women's rights activists, populists, and anyone who has ever believed that happiness can be not only pursued, but attained. But a manifesto is not the same thing as a constitution. The U.S. Constitution lacks the mythic resonances of the Declaration, although it takes little reflection to see that it is the backdrop, if not the foundation, for all American Dreams. Whatever their disagreements about its scope or character, most Americans would agree that their government is legitimate insofar as it permits a level playing field of Dreams. Many of us have doubts that the government *does* serve this function; many fewer have doubts that it *should.*

But the American Dream was alive and well, even if nobody called it as such, long before there was a Constitution, a Declaration, or even a United States of America. The life and autobiography of Benjamin Franklin alone makes that clear (Franklin 1791; Cullen 2003, 60–65). Indeed, as historians of the American Revolution have long asserted, much of the energy for independence, at least initially, was understood as a struggle by the colonists who feared losing an old way of life in a reorganized British empire, not creating a new one. In an important sense, American *society* in many colonies preceded anything resembling a powerful, centralized *government,* and, even after independence, frontier governments had only the most bare-bones civic institutions, much in the manner depicted by yet another HBO series, *Deadwood,* set in a nineteenth-century Dakota Territory mining town.

So I suspect the American Dream is more the product of a cultural environment than a political ideology or a set of political arrangements. The Dream thrived in a monarchy before it did in a republic. And, some might say, the Dream seems to be thriving in a civilization that has long since become an empire. In fact, some might go further and say that the American Dream itself is an imperial construct, a sense of possibility for some that necessarily depends on taking it away from others—in this case, Native Americans, African Americans, and Mexicans, among others.

This view has, of course, considerable cogency. But it may also explain a little too much: As far as I can tell, *every* society has derived its legitimacy through some means of apportioning and distributing opportunity to its members, however broadly or narrowly defined, whether the society in question is that of the ancient Mayans or the presumably egalitarian Soviet Union. And that distribution has usually meant confiscating the resources of others. If we must shed our illusions about the Dream being a uniquely good thing, I think we should also recognize that it has not been uniquely bad.

Like its Roman and other predecessors, the American Dream's power derives from the way it retains its appeal, and extends its dominions, by incorporating those it formerly oppressed even as it maintains its ability to project its political and military power. There is no better illustration of the point than what might be termed the "New Man" of our day, the current president of the United States.

Actually, no one is more aware of his status as an embodiment of the American Dream than that president, who unofficially launched his campaign for higher office in 2006 by publishing *The Audacity of Hope,* a book whose subtitle is *Thoughts on Reclaiming the American Dream.* Obama used the rhetoric and imagery of the American Dream throughout his quest for the presidency, in ways that ranged from campaign rallies to op-ed pieces (Obama 2007). He worked the trope of upward mobility perhaps most effectively in his March 2008 speech in race relations, when he presented himself—as successful candidates typically do—as fusing strands of aspiration:

> I am the son of a black man from Kenya and a white woman from Kansas. I was raised with the help of a white grandfather who survived a Depression to serve in Patton's Army during World War II and a white grandmother who worked on a bomber assembly line at Fort Leavenworth while he was overseas. I've gone to some of the best schools in America and lived in one of the world's poorest nations. I am married to a black American who carries within her the blood of slaves and slave owners—an inheritance we pass on to our two precious daughters. I have brothers, sisters, nieces, nephews, uncles, and cousins, of every race and every hue, scattered across three continents, and for as long as I live, I will never forget that in no other country on Earth is my story even possible. (Obama 2008b)

Regardless of whether his story is possible anywhere else on Earth, Obama presides over a government with the power to project its will everywhere else on the face of the earth. He came to office inheriting two wars in which the United States was widely viewed as a colonial power in all but name, and if he was viewed abroad as a far more moderate figure than his predecessor and one who won office in large measure because he vowed to end those wars (indeed, he was awarded a Nobel Peace Prize, apparently for these reasons), he nevertheless avails himself of the perquisites of his position as he sees fit—which, as it has turned out, means continuing to prosecute these wars.

Again, this is not necessarily a self-evident corruption of the American Dream. Like the Great Emancipator he greatly admires, Obama has cast the projection of power in compellingly moral terms, at home and abroad. "What makes us one American family is that we have to stand up and fight for each other's dreams," he said during his campaign for president. "It's time to reaffirm that fundamental belief—I am my brother's keeper, I am my sister's keeper—through our politics, our policies, and in our daily lives" (Obama 2008a). Or, as he put it in his Nobel Prize acceptance speech (2009), "There will be times when nations—acting individually or in concert—will find the use of force not only necessary but morally justified." As the generations of activists who made his triumph possible know in their bones, one does not always fight for dreams with abstractions or without recourse to the power of the state.

But the real issue we face now may be not how legitimate the American Dream can be in a context of empire but rather how much longer that empire will last. Like a lot of my fellow Americans, I fret that real parallels can be drawn between what we call the late Roman Republic and what is, at least in name, a centuries-old American Republic (shows like *Rome* get produced for a reason, after all). I do not want to exaggerate those parallels. George W. Bush was not Julius Caesar, and Iraq is not Transalpine Gaul. It is a mistake to think that the state of the Union and the problems I and other observers see emerged in 2001; indeed, such analysts as Paul Kennedy (1987) and Kevin Phillips (2002) have identified them as originating decades earlier. Conversely, it does not seem particularly realistic to think that Obama can single-handedly put our national house in order permanently.

I do not want to get bogged down in a highly subjective argument beyond my ken as to what degree the United States is suffering from imperial overstretch—something that was decidedly *not* afflicting the remarkably robust Roman legions in the first century B.C.—at the turn of the twenty-first century. But it takes no great skills of intellectual prognostication to observe that no hegemon lasts forever. American military power will not be eternal. Its political arrangements, always subject to revision, are likely to undergo dramatic changes at some point. Its now postindustrial economic system is in flux (as best). Is there reason to think that the American Dream will endure longer than the United States does?

I believe so. One reason, which a show like *Rome* illuminates, is that values and culture are enormously resilient phenomena and do not necessarily respond in sync with political or economic developments. Moreover, the strongly personal and private dimensions of the American Dream, diffuse and contradictory as they are, are not easily manipulated or even affected by larger events. Indeed, to some extent, they offer a buffer from—even an alternative to—the public square. Who among us, after all, has not reassessed our priorities in the aftermath of a professional setback or a dismaying political development by rededicating ourselves to literal or metaphorical gardens? This focus may not be an altogether satisfactory solution, and, indeed, when large numbers of people turn inward, it can have negative ramifications for a shared culture as a whole. But such a dynamic would certainly be nothing new. In good times and bad, an individualistic version of the American Dream has thrived.

Actually, in some sense, this point goes to the heart of what the American Dream is in its essence: a *culturally* democratic phenomenon. It may not be *qualitatively* different than, say, the Roman Dream of the New Man, but it certainly is *quantitatively* so in terms of the number of people in its purview. And, to go a step further, one might say that the quantity becomes a quality in its own right. (This perhaps more than any other way has made the United States exceptional to the degree that it is.) Nowhere, in the wonderfully apt phrase of Alexis de Tocqueville (1840, 71), has "the charm of anticipated success" been celebrated so much and so widely as in our country—yes, *country*, mind you, not nation. Indeed, we take collective pride in the very fact of its breadth and the belief that such breadth has only grown over time. Who, I must wonder, can be happier about the success of Oprah Winfrey and Obama than white people? Winfrey and Obama are emblems of a Dream redeemed.

To review, then: The American Dream derives from a notion of a better life that is not solely American. Nor does it depend on a republican form of government—indeed, the Dream existed before the republic did, and we have reason to think it will survive that republic (in effect, it may have already done so). But insofar as the sense of human aspiration we have come to call the American Dream has a distinctive flavor, it rests on the breadth of that aspiration and the way it has offered a sense of social cohesion, at times paradoxically, in its most avowedly individualistic incarnations. Even when we have agreed on nothing else, we granted each other the right to dream.

To define the concept this broadly may well prompt a question about what, in the end, the American Dream is *not*. In some sense, that is simple: In feudal states and fundamentalist religious regimes, to cite two examples, politics are rigidly hierarchical, social roles are frozen, and economic transactions are regulated in ways that strangle mobility. In such places, thinking about a different, better life is perhaps inevitable but not viewed as especially realistic or even possible. Yet it is worth remembering that in the American South of the eighteenth century—a society that, if not literally feudal, certainly appeared to be in certain respects—aspiration jostled alongside oppression for blacks and whites alike. Franklin could embody a notion of the Dream in a Pennsylvania where slavery was still legal. "Dreaminess," you might say, is relative and contextual.

But this begs a final question, whose answer is perhaps necessarily subjective but nevertheless worth considering: If the American Dream were dead, how would we know? (I should observe here that its death has been asserted many times, although it also appears to have many more than nine lives.) What kinds of things would we imagine, for example, our politicians would say? And what, if anything, would be likely to take its place? (Actually, I suspect that the word "place," as in being rooted in one and accepting one's lot, would be crucial.) I do not regard the American Dream as an unambiguously good thing. Maybe, if for no other reason than to figure out who and where we are, it is time we imagine the alternatives.

References

Casson, L. 1975. *Everyday life in ancient Rome.* Exp. ed. Baltimore, MD: Johns Hopkins University Press, 1998.

Cullen, J. 2003. *The American Dream: A short history of an idea that shaped a nation.* New York: Oxford University Press.

Franklin, B. 1791. *The autobiography of Benjamin Franklin.* New York: Oxford University Press, 1990.

Harris, R. 2006. *Imperium: A novel of ancient Rome.* New York: Simon and Schuster.

———. 2010. *Conspirata: A novel of ancient Rome.* New York: Simon and Schuster.

Kennedy, P. 1987. *The rise and fall of the great powers: Economic change and military conflict from 1500 to 2000*. New York: Random House.

Murphy, C. 2007. *Are we Rome? The fall of an empire and the fate of America*. Boston: Houghton Mifflin.

Obama, B. 2006. *The audacity of hope: Thoughts on reclaiming the American Dream*. New York: Crown.

——. 2007. *Remarks of Senator Barack Obama: Reclaiming the American Dream*. November 7. Available at www.barackobama.com/2007/11/07/remarks_of _senator_barack_obam_31.php.

——. 2008a. Barack Obama: Reclaiming the American Dream. *Providence Journal*, March 2. Available at www.projo.com/opinion/contributors/content/ CT_obama2_03-02-08_GE95U43_v10.39c783b.html.

——. 2008b. Speech on race (transcript). *New York Times*, March 18. Accessed via nytimes.com.

——. 2009. Obama's Nobel remarks. *New York Times*, December 10. Accessed via nytimes.com.

Phillips, K. 2002. *Wealth and democracy: A political history of the American rich*. New York: Broadway Books.

Rome. Seasons 1 and 2. DVD. HBO Home Video, 2007, 2008.

Saylor, S. 1991. *Roman blood: A novel*. New York: Minotaur.

——. 1993. *Catalina's riddle: A novel*. New York: Minotaur.

Simon, P. Train in the distance. *Hearts and bones*. CD. Warner Brothers Records, 1983.

Tocqueville, A. de. 1840. *Democracy in America*. Vol. II. Henry Reeve text, revised by Francis Bowen, corrected and edited by Phillips Bradley. New York: Vintage Books, 1990.

CHAPTER 2

The Politics of the American Dream, 1980 to 2008

Michael C. Kimmage

THE AMERICAN DREAM has physics and metaphysics, a material and a spiritual component. The material component concerns wealth or well-being, with citizenship shading into ownership: One steps closer to the American Dream by buying a house or owning a car. The material component suggests class mobility or simply the pleasure of economic opportunity, a motive for immigration to America as long as there have been immigrants. The spiritual component, the metaphysics of the American Dream, is a blend of optimism and happiness, alluded to in the Declaration of Independence, in which happiness is a thing to be pursued. The American Dream could be defined as the spiritualization of property and consumption, the investment of joy and dignity in consumption and property ownership. The aristocrat would disdain this spiritualization; the Christian ascetic would fear it; and the socialist would claim that it reinforces the power of the propertied classes. In America, it is embraced. In no country is the voyage into the middle class and upper-middle class as intoxicating as it is in America, whatever statistics may say about the country's actual class structure, actual poverty levels, and actual stagnation of opportunity. The American Dream promises immediate property and ultimate happiness, physical possessions, consumer goods, and an ensuing metaphysical joy.[1]

---

[1] A helpful overview of the American dream as an idea or image in American history is Jim Cullen, *The American Dream: A Short History of an Idea that Shaped a Nation* (New York: Oxford University Press, 2003).

The metaphysics of the American Dream help tell a political story concentrated in the years between 1980 and 2008. One could use the following somewhat tautological axiom as a thesis statement: The political party in closer touch with the American Dream is more likely to acquire and to hold on to power. The same cultural aspirations that aided Ronald Reagan in 1980 later aided Barack Obama in 2008.

One part of this story is the rise of the Republican Party, with Reagan as its leader; another part is the decline of the New Deal coalition put together in the 1930s; and the third part is the election of Obama. In the twelve years between 1980 and 1992, the entire political spectrum in the United States was moved to the right, a national trend that began in 1980 and was consolidated by Bill Clinton, a Democratic president and pro-business progressive who declared that the "era of big government is over" (Clinton 1996).[2] Clinton, a legendarily canny politician, bid farewell to orthodoxies that had guided the Democratic Party for some fifty years. If he did not wish to emulate Reagan, he was not above learning from a Republican master who had forged a winning connection between the Republican Party and the American Dream. Jimmy Carter in 1980, Walter Mondale in 1984, and Michael Dukakis in 1988—three losing Democratic contenders for the White House—had failed to harmonize the American Dream with the language and the policies of their party. They worried their way to defeat. Reagan embodied optimism about the American economy and the American future. Clinton embodied optimism, too, but he had to reverse the policies of his party to make it politically credible. Only by reducing the size of government and by blessing the virtues of consumption could Clinton benefit from the metaphysics of the American Dream. The politics of the American Dream, from 1980 to 2000, mandated optimism about the American future and enthusiasm about American-style capitalism. In 2008, with the economy in shambles and a charismatic Democrat in ascendancy, the Right finally lost its grip.

The Democratic Party's argument with the American Dream, circa 1980, has a long prehistory. What 1980 was to the Republican Party, 1932 was to the Democratic Party, the moment a charismatic leader came into his own and the moment when a new political coalition came into its own. Despite his rejection of Franklin Roosevelt's political ideas, Reagan greatly admired the Democratic president who ruled midcen-

---

[2] Clinton made this resonant statement in a 1996 radio broadcast.

tury American politics. Reagan's was the admiration of one professional for another, Reagan and Roosevelt being not just professional politicians but professional optimists; and Roosevelt's optimism was indeed remarkable. Roosevelt's biography was no rags-to-riches story; he was not a classic product of the American Dream. Almost a European aristocrat, born to wealth and privilege, Roosevelt was not someone who had to work his way through Harvard but someone destined to attend Harvard, as he did. Yet Roosevelt had a genuine common touch. His access to the American Dream, to the striving associated with the phrase, was not a matter of class but of physical tribulation. He contracted polio and persevered. His spirit was undaunted, and his striving seemed less like political ambition and more like the striving of common Americans trying to grasp their national Dream. Roosevelt had earned the optimism that was his trademark as a politician, conveyed by his famous smile, by his fluency with public speaking, and by his relationship with what became an admiring nation. Roosevelt was optimistic and cheerful when few contemporary political figures were: Joseph Stalin and Adolf Hitler did not exude optimism and good cheer. Even Winston Churchill, Roosevelt's ally, was an advocate of tough-minded pessimism and of facing up to the terrifying truth of Nazi and Soviet aggression and was no apostle of optimism.[3]

Roosevelt was an optimist in hard times. His optimism carried a political message: Liberal democracy can survive; the American system can survive; and the American Dream, whether physical or metaphysical, need not be discarded. Nevertheless, the hardness of the hard times was fundamental to Roosevelt's political career. The Great Depression began in 1929, during the presidency of Herbert Hoover, and Roosevelt came to power in 1932, in large part because he was alert to the experience of hard times. Hoover had tried to be optimistic as a Depression-era president; he had tried to stave off panic and to emphasize that economic downturns were often short-lived. His optimism is now proverbial for its inadequacy. Roosevelt offered the recipe of greater government involvement to a nation with widespread unemployment, with a financial sector in crisis, and with its agriculture and economy moving in downward spirals. The key to the New Deal was the desperation of the

---

[3] A brilliant essay on Roosevelt's optimism as a deviation from the politics of his times is Isaiah Berlin's "President Franklin Delano Roosevelt," in *Personal Impressions,* ed. Henry Hardy (Princeton, NJ: Princeton University Press, 2001), 24–33.

average citizen, and Hoover had no language for addressing this desperation, while Roosevelt did. In 1937, in FDR's second inaugural, a speech where lesser presidents might simply have trumpeted the achievements of their first terms, he spoke with candor:

> Here is the challenge to our democracy: In this nation I see tens of millions of its citizens—a substantial part of its whole population—who at this very moment are denied the greater part of what the very lowest standards of today call the necessities of life. I see millions of families trying to live on incomes so meager that the pall of family disaster hangs over them day by day. I see millions whose daily lives in city and on farm continue under conditions labeled indecent by a so-called polite society half a century ago. I see millions denied education, recreation, and the opportunity to better their lot and the lot of their children. I see millions lacking the means to buy the products of farm and factory and by their poverty denying work and productiveness to many other millions. I see one-third of a nation ill-housed, ill-clad, ill-nourished. (Roosevelt 1937)

These are vivid images of family poverty; but the spirit of the words denies the necessity of such poverty and implies that something has gotten in the way of American normalcy. Then Roosevelt the politician turned this image into an argument for the New Deal:

> It is not in despair that I paint you that picture. I paint it for you in hope—because the nation, seeing and understanding the injustice in it, proposes to paint it out. We are determined to make every American citizen the subject of his country's interest and concern; and we will never regard any faithful law-abiding group within our borders as superfluous. The test of our progress is not whether we add more to the abundance of those who have much; it is whether we provide enough for those who have too little. (Ibid.)

Roosevelt downplayed the metaphysics of the American Dream; he did not spin phrases about the joys of owning property, about the happiness that emanates from home and car and from the efforts made to acquire them. These pleasures were too far from the reality of the Great Depression, even if they remained an object of desire for many Americans. Roosevelt concentrated on the physics of the American Dream, especially on employment as its lifeblood, and he did so with an optimism that was provisional. The American Dream would come in the future, when the Depression was over. In the interim, the president's policies bespoke a crisis of political economy. The New Deal coalition, which lasted for decades, was born in hard times, when for many the American Dream was a Dream deferred.

Superficially, the 1970s bore some resemblance to the 1930s. The postwar prosperity that overtook the United States and Western Europe started to ebb in the early 1970s. The French call the thirty years after World War II *les trentes glorieuses,* the thirty glorious years, a glory drained by the global energy crisis and the attendant economic stagnation. As in the 1930s, the specter of a dark future loomed. It was a good time for pessimists, who could point to the American defeat in Vietnam, to the Watergate scandal, to the drying up of good jobs, to the degradation of the environment, and to the vulgarity of American culture in the 1970s and predict that worse was yet to come. If the 1970s were like the 1930s, then the old recipes might be in demand once again. Was this not a time for a new FDR, who could preside by extending the beneficent hand of government, by enlarging the safety net and asserting the regulatory impulse previously used to control the robber barons and now needed to control renegade corporations? A more modest word than "depression" hovered around Carter and the late 1970s. Carter implied that America was living through a period of malaise, and he offered no ultimate optimism. The word "malaise" came to haunt his presidency, as did the sense that, unlike FDR, he had no recipe for hard times. He may still have had the New Deal coalition behind him, a collection of voters accustomed to supporting the Democratic Party, but his presidency was harried and difficult, taking on the coloration of a final chapter and not of a new beginning. Americans could look at Carter and feel that the American Dream was either destined to break apart, a casualty of malaise, or that the American Dream was itself a participant in the malaise. The ceaseless material advancement was too expensive, too harmful, and even vaguely immoral. Carter turned down the heat in the White House and sold the presidential yacht. The symbolism was not intended to be esoteric.

Carter lost to Reagan in 1980 for many reasons. A subtle one involved Carter's public worries about the American Dream. Carter did not have FDR's talent for balancing optimism and pessimism. The crisis of the 1970s was smaller than that of the 1930s, and behind it was a very recent memory of booming prosperity, of an economic expansion almost without historical precedent; but Carter could only see difficulties ahead of him. A conservative political movement had been developing long before 1980, with the explicit ambition of shattering the New Deal legacy. Born in hard times, the New Deal coalition itself fell on hard times in the 1970s. Slowly, the Democratic Party had grown more backward-looking than forward-thinking, orienting itself less around future Dreams than around future anxieties: If past achievements were forgotten, if the New Deal safety net were undone, the future might be truly dark. After the revolutionary heyday of the 1960s, the American Left discovered pessimism in the 1970s: Carter's moderate pessimism and, further to his left, a pessimism about the intractable racism and inequality of middle-class American life as well as an apocalyptic pessimism about the environment. In 1980, Reagan's emotional anti-Communism helped get him elected, but no less important was Reagan's access to the American Dream in the domain of domestic politics. While Carter was distancing the Left from the American Dream, Reagan worked to associate the American Dream with conservatism and the Republican Party.

The physics of the American Dream, the actual state of the economy during the Reagan presidency, was ambiguous. In part, the eighties was a prosperous decade. Many enjoyed the affluence, and it was implicit to Reaganomics that consumption would and should drive economic expansion. Under Reagan, the heat in the White House was presumably turned back up. If Reagan did not buy back the presidential yacht, he allowed himself a lavish inauguration in 1981 that made a mockery of Carter's austerity. Nancy Reagan's expensive dresses graced a new White House, the resplendent terminus for an American Dream that Reagan could easily represent. He had grown up in a poor Illinois family, a child of the Depression, the son of an alcoholic, and became wealthy by virtue of his talents, first in Hollywood and then as a spokesman for General Electric. Roosevelt may have *felt* closer to America's poor—he may have shown them greater empathy and believed that their concerns were the concerns of the federal government—but Reagan *came* from poverty. Therefore, his wealth had the sanction of the American Dream. This was only one story line from the Reagan years. The other story line was one of poverty and relative hopelessness. The bottom third of the economy was in shambles. A confluence of poverty, drug abuse, racial segregation, and urban decline yielded a special kind of American misery, visible on the streets of Detroit; Philadelphia; Los Angeles; and, indeed, of Washington, D.C., in the 1980s. Classically, the American Dream promised what Europe could not deliver: greater prosperity for greater numbers, chances that could be more easily claimed in the New World than elsewhere. Yet the inner-city poverty of the 1980s was worse than the poverty of Western Europe, the blight more severe. The American Dream is a doctrine of progress: The physics of the American Dream, in the late twentieth century, clearly reflected progress and decline.

Reagan excelled at the metaphysics of the American Dream. His biography was one part of the equation. His rhetoric was a greater part. His was a conservatism that could accommodate progress, a conservatism with no antipathy for modern America, no antipathy for technology, no antipathy for capitalism, and no antipathy for the dynamics of change. Reagan could be pessimistic, but it was a pessimism that underscored the optimism of his social vision: He was pessimistic about the federal government, labeling government the problem, not the solution. The ills of the 1970s, to which Reagan was no less sensitive than the gloom-ridden Carter, were the ills of over-government, in Reagan's eyes, an over-involvement of government in the lives of individuals, of too many burdens placed on the shoulders of the free market, weighing down the public and private sectors alike. FDR had promised that government could right the wrongs of the free market and renew the American Dream for average Americans. Reagan reversed the argument: Government stood in the way of the American Dream, and scaling back the role of government would only bring Americans closer to achieving their Dreams. Reagan's understanding of the American Dream was grounded in the individual, not in government. The size of government had to be reduced for the sake of individual self-improvement. Reagan's optimistic individualism, which was and is enormously popular, outlines a paradox at the heart of the American Dream. Although it is by definition a national Dream, the agent of the American Dream is not really the nation: It is a Dream dreamt by a nation of individuals.

In the 1990s, the Democratic Party reclaimed the White House, recapturing the individualistic American Dream with Bill Clinton. If the crises of the 1970s recalled those of the 1930s, the giddy money making of the 1990s suggested a repetition of the Roaring Twenties. Both decades—the 1920s and the 1990s—were golden ages for the American Dream. Under Clinton, a technological revolution dovetailed with dramatic economic growth; the resulting conspicuous consumption was yet another enactment of the American Dream. Once again, the metaphysics of the American Dream obscured the physics, as the bottom half of the economy either benefited little from the boom or descended into greater indebtedness and insecurity. In political terms, Clinton could profit from the Dream's brilliant metaphysics—with Bill Gates its patron saint in the 1990s—without lingering over the problems beneath its surface. He did not struggle to save the country from malaise or crisis—he was fortunate in this regard—but his good fortune was also a repudiation of his party's history. Clinton was a new kind of Democrat. From Carter's failure and Reagan's success, Clinton had learned how politically crucial the metaphysics of the American Dream is, what price one pays for denying it, and what one can win by presenting oneself as a spokesman and specimen of the American Dream—presenting oneself as the poor boy from Hope, Arkansas, who had studied and worked his way to the presidency. Clinton put an end to the New Deal coalition by putting an end to the New Deal mentality, in which the American Dream was often a Dream deferred, with government as the long-term medium for bringing the American Dream to the citizen. An aura of crisis had inspired a socialization of the American Dream, as it had the notion of the American Dream as delayed gratification. Whether a Democrat or Republican was in office, by the year 2000, the political drift was toward the immediate and the individual, a tendency encouraged by bipartisan appeals to the American Dream. The Dream had become economic fact, the political establishment seemed to be saying, and it was the job of the governing party to cultivate and to advertise this fact.

The 2000 presidential election, which was among the strangest in American history, was not about the American Dream. It was curiously passionless at the time, without sharp issues and vivid personalities. It was also famously inconclusive, with the new president seeming to descend from the will of the Supreme Court rather than from the wellspring of popular sovereignty. In no obvious way did its winner embody the American Dream. George W. Bush, for all the Texan American-ness of his persona, was almost European in his dynastic claim on the White House, an inheritor first of wealth, then of position, then of the executive privileges that came with the Bush family name. Additionally, the events of September 11 dominated Bush's administration, and in the wake of this trauma Bush failed to articulate a vision beyond fear: His optimism about projecting the American Dream into the Middle East, of bringing democracy and prosperity to Iraq, was shown to be a false and possibly a phony optimism. His domestic policies were nondescript and darkened eventually by the economic crisis that began in the final months of his presidency. Bush had neither a biography nor an agenda in coherent harmony with the American Dream, something especially evident when September 11 fears started to dissipate in his second term. Here, the symbolism of Hurricane Katrina is significant. The government's incompetence was certainly damaging to the Bush administration, and it cast a retrospective shadow over America's post–September 11 foreign policy; perhaps the government had been as clumsy overseas as it was proving to be at home. More acutely, the images broadcast from the Gulf States, and especially from the city of New Orleans, were a repudiation of the American Dream, evidence that the American Dream—as embodied in property ownership—could be undone, first by nature and then by some deficiency of communal effort. Much of the property destroyed in the hurricane and flood was not the property Americans dreamed of owning: This, too, was put on display by the hurricane. To the extent that Bush neither personified nor defended the American Dream, his presidency was perceived to be a failure.

In no sense, however, did the American Dream die with Bush's presidency.

At times, the brilliant personalities of the 2008 presidential campaign, from Sarah Palin to Obama, could obscure the election's grim socioeconomic framework. The economic crisis had begun in 2007, if not considerably earlier, although until September 2008, it was not the election's inevitable theme. By the fall of 2008, the economic crisis had become visible and unavoidable. Those at the apex of the American Dream were somehow at the center of a massive instability. Their avenue to wealth had not been the mythic application of thrift and discipline, from which society might profit as well. Many had been speculating with others' money, using complex mathematical models to guarantee their wealth, without knowing (or wishing to know) the degree of risk they were imposing upon the country at large. Their Dream was faltering in public view, in the fall of 2008, repudiating the promises Republican and Democratic presidents (such as Clinton) had made about the global economy. As with Katrina, the symbol of this economic crisis was home ownership, that cornerstone of the American Dream. (One might contrast this to September 11, in which offices, military and business, were first destroyed and then passionately defended.) American homes were not worth as much in October as they had been in August; many Americans could not afford the homes they had bought, causing the rate of foreclosure to increase dramatically; and speculators had pushed home loans on American dreamers who would have been better off renting or buying smaller homes. The progressive nature of the American Dream—more homes, more value, more opportunity—ran up against a bitter reality at just the moment Americans were going to the polls. At no time since the Second World War had the physics of the American Dream been so bad.

The economic crisis arrived too late in the campaigning season for either candidate to respond comprehensively to it. The election was fought more on the terrain of the Dream's metaphysics. John McCain had his own American narrative, the narrative of a George Washington or a Ulysses S. Grant or a Dwight Eisenhower, of military valor turned into political prestige, even if McCain had never been a general. He was a military hero, but McCain was also born into a respected military family. Impeccable as his American credentials were, his biography said little about the American Dream and much about the qualities required for protecting it. Palin, his running mate, could be fit into the American Dream's eternal narrative. She had several of its classic attributes: Her family name was entirely unknown, she had not studied at a great university, she lived in a provincial American town, and she had risen almost immediately from mayor to governor. Palin possessed the populist elements implicit to the American Dream, its association of simplicity and humble origins with the glorious chance to transcend these origins. Nevertheless, she struggled to convince the American electorate that she had earned her invitation to high office. The myth of the American Dream is a myth of hard work rewarded, and several stages seemed to be missing from Palin's journey on her path from the mayor of Wasilla, Alaska, to the White House. During the election, the popular parodies of Palin were also parodies of the American Dream, a burlesque version of its mathematics, whereby labor and talent are the building blocks of success. If a fool could rise to the heights of American power, perhaps the vaunted American Dream was a fool's Dream. This *Saturday Night Live* joke had as its historical context all the blows struck against the American Dream, from Hurricane Katrina to the economic crisis. On the terrain of the American Dream, neither McCain nor Palin could compete with Obama.

With Obama, the American Dream took on a different meaning, or he brought a new element to its meaning. More than a decade before running for president, Obama had written a book about the American Dream, which he first published in 1995 and titled *Dreams from My Father*. In its candor and scope, it is among America's most unusual political biographies. Not all the Dreams in *Dreams from My Father* are American Dreams. Indeed, Obama's father was not an American citizen, but a Kenyan who dreamt of going to America and who realized his Dream by attending the University of Hawaii. There he met a white American woman and had a child who become America's president in 2009. The first American dream, in *Dreams from My Father,* stems from the father's dreams—that is, the dream of coming to America, a dream with universal implications. Obama's father was fond of discussing "the promise of the American dream" (Obama 2004, 21). The second American Dream, in this book, is found outside America, in Indonesia, where Obama spent part of his childhood. In Indonesia, Obama's mother pushed him not to become a fatalist, not to succumb to others' low expectations, but to act upon his own destiny; his mother understood this action as distinctly American and more as a spiritual (metaphysical) than an acquisitive endeavor. The personal battle between action, effort, and education is the drama of this autobiography, whose protagonist succumbs at times to fatalism and self-destructiveness only to return to the battleground of self-making and self-advancement, progressing step by step to a position of national prominence. This journey began with a question that the young Obama asked of himself: "Don't you know who I am?" To this question, after years of existential uncertainty, he was ultimately able to answer: "I'm an *individual*" (Ibid., 101; emphasis original). Once again, it is the individual who dreams a nation's Dream.

The first of these Dreams is the father's Dream of American opportunity, palpable in Kenya as it is within the United States; the second is the American son's Dream of individual labor; and the third is Martin Luther King's Dream of racial equality, "Dr. King's magnificent dream," as Obama calls it in *Dreams from My Father* (Ibid., 30). In his inaugural address, Obama offered himself as a fulfillment of King's Dream, standing at the opposite end of the National Mall from the place where King had delivered his "I Have a Dream" speech in 1963. A Dream fulfilled had not been promised to Obama when he was a young black man in America. Obama was born in 1961 to a mixed-race family. He did not experience legal segregation firsthand, and he was able to study at Columbia University, thereby entering into the professional classes. An elite university made a wealth accessible to Obama that was inaccessible to his white mother or to her white parents. No terrible limits had been placed upon his career or on his American horizons. Yet the African American world around him still betrayed the trauma of America's racial history and a fatalism reinforced in vicious cycles of black poverty. As a student in New York, Obama came to know the confining connection between race and "the ladder into the American dream," the hard calculus of prejudice, poverty, education, and professional possibility arranged street by street in New York City (Ibid., 164). The white American's Dream is not the same as the black American's Dream, precisely the problem King had used to structure his "I Have a Dream" speech.

Dreams from My Father, its sober report on racial inequality balanced by its saga of triumphant individual will, is the book that launched Obama's career in national politics.

The 2008 election cannot be reduced to Obama's American Dreams. Voters may be voting for a Dream, but most likely they are voting for interests, for ideology, and for the intricate matters of public and foreign policy that inform legislation and governance. Or voters may pursue negative aims, softening their dislike for a candidate into an appreciation of lesser-evil logic. The interests can be measured, and they figure in the election-day polling, which is anything but reassuringly empirical. Although metaphysical Dreams cannot be measured at all, they play a more-than-impressionistic role. It would be absurd to deny the power of Obama's story, whether on the printed page or as the frame for a well-organized presidential campaign. Obama could represent and broaden the American Dream; he could speak for it, and his election could show, to Americans and to the world, that the American Dream was not given to one race and denied to another. As before, the political currency of the American Dream is optimism. The Obama campaign's emphasis on hope and its mantra of "yes we can" were statements of optimism translated into the language of mass politics. In the improbable months, starting with the Iowa Caucus in January 2008, in which Obama triumphed first over Hillary Clinton and then over McCain, Obama was able to align his message of optimism with a winning constituency of voters, putting him on par with FDR and Reagan in the effectiveness of his method. Like FDR and Reagan, Obama had mastered the metaphysics of the American Dream. As with FDR and Reagan, the challenges of Obama's presidency will revolve not around the metaphysics of the American Dream but around the far-less-changeable variables of its Earth-bound physics.

References

Clinton, B. 1996. *The era of big government is over: Radio address.* January 27. Available at www.cnn.com/US/9601/budget/01-27/clinton_radio/.

Obama, B. 2004. *Dreams from my father: A story of race and inheritance.* New York: Three Rivers Press.

Roosevelt, F. D. 1937. *Second inaugural address.* January 20. Available at http://avalon.law.yale.edu/20th_century/froos2.asp.

CHAPTER 3

The Presidency and the Making of the American Dream

John Kenneth White

JANUARY 20, 2009: It was a day of celebration, vindication, and doubt. The celebration came as Democrats rejoiced to see one of their own, Barack Obama, become the nation's forty-fourth president after eight long years of being shut out of Republican George W. Bush's White House. It was also a day of vindication, as African Americans could tell their children that they, like Obama, could aspire to the nation's highest office. And it was a day of doubt, as Americans collectively wondered whether they (and their new president) could overcome the most serious economic crisis since the Great Depression or whether the United States had entered a long, steep decline in which its best days were past.

Obama captured all three of these sentiments during his two-year-long quest for the presidency. From the start of his campaign in 2007, Obama understood that one of the most important functions of any chief executive is to "speak American," as former Bill Clinton speech-writer David Kusnet so memorably stated (Kusnet 1992). For Obama, that meant paying homage to the American Dream and using his personal story to illustrate its staying power. Writing in his 2006 book, *The Audacity of Hope: Thoughts on Reclaiming the American Dream,* Obama linked the American Dream to the many positive attributes associated with freedom: self-reliance, self-improvement, risk taking, drive, discipline, temperance, hard work, thrift, and personal responsibility. Obama declared that these values "are rooted in a basic optimism about life and a faith in free will—a confidence that through pluck and sweat and smarts, each of us can rise above the circumstances of our birth" (Obama 2006, 54). As a presidential candidate, Obama returned time and again to three simple ideas: (1) The American Dream is real; (2) the values it espouses are eternal; and (3) although presently under duress, the American Dream could be revived once more. As Obama so memorably expressed it from his first arrival on the national stage at the Democratic National Convention in 2004, "I stand here knowing that my story is part of the larger American story, that I owe a debt to all of those who came before me, and that in no other country on Earth is my story even possible" (Obama 2004b).

Even in his first moments as president-elect, Obama cast his 2008 victory not as a triumph of one man but as a ratification of the American Dream: "If there is anyone out there who still doubts that America is a place where all things are possible, who still wonders if the dream of our founders is alive in our time, who still questions the power of our democracy, tonight is your answer" (Obama 2008b). These words had particular resonance for African Americans. Campaign manager David Plouffe remembered being struck on election night when he left his office and took an elevator to the lobby of a Chicago high-rise on his way to meet the new president. Upon being spotted by the security guards—all of them African Americans—he was greeted with spontaneous and heartfelt applause. Reflecting on this scene (and similar ones that occurred once Obama's victory was announced), Plouffe wrote that these reactions were "a kind of primal joy at seeing wrongs righted, at having risen up to achieve something cynics said couldn't be done" (Plouffe 2009, 2). Even Obama's erstwhile opponent, John McCain, took notice: "This was an historic election, and I recognize the special significance it has for African Americans and for the special pride that must be theirs tonight" (McCain 2008). Basking in victory, Obama became something much larger than merely another ambitious candidate who had successfully sought the presidency: He became the embodiment of the American Dream itself.

Despite the celebrations following the 2008 election, Obama's inaugural address also captured the whiff of self-doubt that had gripped the nation in the final days of the Bush administration. Obama believed the recession created a malaise that spawned doubts about the American Dream: "Less measurable but no less profound is a sapping of confidence across our land, a nagging fear that America's decline is inevitable, that the next generation must lower its sights" (Obama 2009a). Such self-doubt, particularly misgivings expressed by a president, was rare for much of the twentieth century. In 1941, Henry Luce, the founder of the *Time-Life* publishing empire, heralded the dawn of an "American century" in which the United States was "the dynamic center of ever-widening spheres of enterprise . . . [and a] powerhouse of the ideals of Freedom and Justice" (Luce 1941).

But barely into the twenty-first century, many wondered whether the "American century" had come to an abrupt and premature end. Double-digit unemployment—coupled with a widespread feeling that the federal government was helping big shots rather than ordinary citizens—gave way to a sense that the American Dream had shrunk. Speaking in Iowa on the eve of his victory in the caucuses there, Obama declared: "When our fellow Americans are denied the American Dream, our own dreams are diminished. And today, the cost of that dream is rising faster than ever before. While some have prospered beyond imagination in this global economy, middle-class Americans—as well as those working hard to become middle class—are seeing the American Dream slip further and further away" (Obama 2007). The inference was clear: Electing Obama would reclaim and revitalize the American Dream once more.

Despite a prevailing belief that the American Dream is moving away from the reach of broad segments of American society, even as the president struggles to regain the nation's economic footing, faith in the American Dream still endures—despite the triumphs and failures associated with the U.S. presidency. That steadfast faith in the American Dream is something modern-day presidents (and would-be presidents) have used to find common ground with their fellow citizens.

Dreamers and Presidents

Obama is hardly the first U.S. president to use the powerful imagery of the American Dream to advance his cause. Accepting the Republican presidential nomination in 1960, Richard M. Nixon told the delegates, "I believe in the American Dream because I have seen it come true in my own life" (Nixon 1960). Eight years later, Nixon embellished his personal story by casting himself as the American Dream's tribune:

> I see [a] child tonight. He hears a train go by. At night, he dreams of faraway places where he'd like to go. It seems like an impossible

dream. But he is helped on his journey through life. A father who had to go to work before he finished the sixth grade sacrificed everything so his sons could go to college.

A gentle Quaker mother with a passionate concern for peace quietly wept when he went to war, but she understood why he had to go.

A great teacher, a remarkable football coach, an inspirational minister encouraged him on his way. A courageous wife and loyal children stood by him in victory and also in defeat.

And in his chosen profession of politics, first there were scores, then hundreds, then thousands, and finally millions who worked for his success.

And tonight he stands before you, nominated for president of the United States of America.

You can see why I believe so deeply in the American Dream. (Nixon 1968)

Nixon biographer Tom Wicker wrote that Nixon's political potency lay not in his achievements and failures as president; rather, it was that many voters saw Nixon as "one of us." In his book *One of Us: Richard Nixon and the American Dream,* the former *New York Times* columnist wrote that in Nixon Americans recognized "their own sentimental patriotism and confidence in national virtue, their professed love of God and family, their theological belief that hard work would pay off, their desire to get ahead and live well, their preference for action over reflection—hardhead over egghead—and their vocal if not always practiced devotion to freedom and democracy" (Wicker 1991, 686).

As Nixon's political odyssey so amply illustrates, U.S. presidents are powerful exponents of the American Dream, because they embody the aspirations of their fellow citizens in a way no other public official can possibly match. An 1844 newspaper editorial declared that presidents "serve as an example that honest labor is not degrading and that the highest civic honors are within the reach of the industrious and the persevering" (Pessen 1984, 1–2). As the late political scientist Clinton Rossiter once observed, "The final greatness of the presidency lies in the truth that it is not just an office of incredible power but a breeding ground of indestructible myth" (Rossiter 1960, 103).

These myths exemplify the American Dream itself. From the inception of the presidency, Americans have associated it with the moral lessons that hard work and virtuous character yield great rewards that give the American Dream a powerful authenticity. At the constitutional convention in Philadelphia, delegates extolled George Washington for his virtue and the lessons that ordinary citizens could derive from his example. This emphasis on Washington's honor led many to grant the presidency more powers than they had been otherwise inclined. As South Carolina delegate Pierce Butler later wrote, "Entre nous, I do [not] believe they [the executive powers] would have been so great had not many of the members cast their eyes toward General Washington as President; and shaped their Ideas of the Powers to be given a President, by their opinions of his Virtue" (Thach 1969, 153). Luther Martin, a delegate to Maryland's ratifying convention, welcomed the prospect of a Washington presidency: "The name of Washington is far above my praise! I would to Heaven that on this occasion one more wreath had been added to the number of those which are twined around his amiable brow—that those with which it is already surrounded may flourish with immortal verdure, not wither or fade till time shall be no more, is my fervent prayer!" (Flexner 1974, 210). It was not that Martin anticipated Washington's actions—no one really could do that; rather, it was Washington's character and his personification of an American Dream fulfilled that really mattered.

Washington is not the only president from which Americans can derive important moral lessons in their personal quests to achieve the American Dream. In 1864, while seeking reelection in the midst of a bloody civil war, Abraham Lincoln was depicted in several "popular life" biographies as an exemplar of what a poor boy can be if he wants "to climb the heights" (Sandburg 1954, 661). For his part, Lincoln embraced the American Dream not just for himself but for everyone: "The penniless beginner in the world labors for wages awhile, saves a surplus with which to buy tools or land for himself; then labors on his own account another while, and at length hires another new beginner to help him." As Lincoln described it, this steady, gradual advance is "the prosperous system, which opens the way for all—gives hope to all, and energy, and progress, and improvement of condition to all" (Von Drehle 2009, 36).

This steady advancement of citizens and presidents of which Lincoln spoke continues to this day. Political hagiographers always stress a potential president's relatively humble origins, even though these stories are often more fictional than factual. As historian Edward Pessen has written: "The venerable American Dream that any boy can rise to the presidency if he displays what James Bryce called the necessary 'merit' turns out to be an illusion—unless merit is defined to mean having parents and grandparents whose standing, wealth, and influence help open doors to success in life" (Pessen 1984, 170–171). Pessen adds that these mythical stories often transform chancy presidential candidates into safe ones, since touting the American Dream and perpetuating the log cabin myth makes these prospective chief magistrates more acceptable to the voters (ibid., 171).

It is not surprising that, once in office, presidents continue to pay homage to the American Dream. Immediately after Ronald Reagan became president in 1981, his pollster Richard Wirthlin advised, "[By] symbolizing the past and future greatness of America and radiating inspirational confidence, a president can pull a nation together while directing its people toward fulfillment of the American Dream" (Wirthlin 1981). As president, Reagan held out hope that the American Dream remained a universal aspiration, even in challenging economic times. At a 1983 press conference, he declared, "What I want to see above all is that this country remains a country where someone can always get rich" (Reagan 1983).

Political scientist Walter Dean Burnham once likened Reagan to a *pontifex maximus*—that is, a president who not only embodies the American Dream in his or her persona but is expected to ratify it in nearly all public pronouncements (Burnham 1989, 6). Burnham added that faith in the American Dream means that president must project a "credible optimism" (ibid., 7). Franklin Roosevelt was just such a president, telling a country "dying by inches" (Roosevelt 1995, 9) thanks to the Great Depression, "This great Nation will endure as it has endured, will revive, and will prosper" (Roosevelt 1933). According to FDR biographer Jonathan Alter, Roosevelt's optimism derived from several "inner islands of strength" that gave him an "emotional intelligence" and created images of comfort in which he took refuge (Alter 2006, 25).

Reagan also had a similar inner confidence and projected a Roosevelt-like optimism to his audience. According to Reagan biographer Lou Cannon, "This optimism was not a trivial or peripheral quality. It was the essential ingredient of an approach to life that had carried Reagan from the backwater of Dixon to fame as a sports announcer and then to the stages of Hollywood and of the world" (Cannon 1991, 26). As one screenwriter recalled, "You get a feeling that everything is going to be all right from him" (ibid., 226). Added Cannon, the feeling that "'everything is going to be all right' . . . would be his most distinctive quality as president" (ibid.).

Indeed, the very first opinion polls taken on the American Dream showed a strong public connection between it and optimistic chief executives. When people were asked in 1986, "Which individual, either living or dead, famous or not famous, exemplifies your idea of the American Dream?" four of the nine most popular responses named a U.S. president:

John F. Kennedy, 8 percent
Abraham Lincoln, 6 percent
Lee Iacocca (chairman and CEO of Chrysler Corporation),
    4 percent
Martin Luther King, 5 percent
Ronald Reagan, 4 percent
My father, 5 percent
Family member (other than father), 6 percent
John Wayne (the late actor), 1 percent
Franklin Delano Roosevelt, 1 percent[1]

In the years after Reagan left the White House, his successors quickly caught on to a vital element of his success by focusing on the American Dream and linking it to commonly held public values—including family, freedom, opportunity, responsibility, self-reliance, and hard work. Accepting the Republican nomination in 1988, Reagan's vice president, George H. W. Bush, cast his life story in a manner that captured the essence of an American Dream fulfilled: "Now [Barbara and I] moved to west Texas forty years ago. . . . We lived in a little shotgun house, one room for the three of us. Worked in the oil business, then started my own. In time we had six children. Moved from the shotgun, to a duplex apartment, to a house. And lived the dream—high school football on Friday night, Little League, neighborhood barbecue" (George H. W. Bush 1988). Four years later, Clinton vividly described his humble upbringing in Hope, Arkansas, and the values lessons he learned while growing up there:

---

[1] *Wall Street Journal*, poll, October 1986. Other responses include no one, 2 percent; other, 23 percent; don't know/no answer, 35 percent. Respondents were given ten seconds to choose someone. Lee Iacocca appears in the poll, because in 1984 he published his very popular autobiography titled *Iacocca: A Biography* (New York: Bantam Books, 1984).

When I think about opportunity for all Americans, I think about my grandfather. He ran a country store in our little town of Hope. There was no food stamps back then, so when his customers, whether they were white or black, who worked hard and did the best they could, came in with no money, well, he gave them food anyway. . . . My grandfather just had a high school education—a grade school education—but in that country store he taught me more about equality in the eyes of the Lord than all my professors at Georgetown, more about the intrinsic worth of every individual than all the philosophers at Oxford, more about the need for equal justice under the law than all the jurists at Yale Law School. . . . My fellow Americans, . . . I still believe in a place called Hope. (Clinton 1992)

Introducing himself to the electorate in 2000, George W. Bush realized the political potency of the American Dream and, like his father, embraced it. Hailing from Midland, Texas, Bush told voters that the town's motto read, "The sky's the limit," adding, "The largest lesson I learned in Midland still guides me: Everyone, from immigrant to entrepreneur, has an equal claim on this country's promise" (George W. Bush 2000).

Obama also looked to Reagan's optimism as an inspiration for setting the tone of his White House years. Speaking before an editorial board of the *Reno Gazette* during the 2008 primary campaign, Obama noted that Reagan "tapped into what people were already feeling, which was we want clarity, we want optimism, we want a return to that sense of dynamism and entrepreneurship that had been missing."[2] At an early juncture in his presidency, Obama described himself as "the eternal optimist," adding, "That's the kind of leadership I'm going to try to provide" (Obama 2009b). Implicit in Obama's comment was an understanding that presidents who fail to project an eternal optimism are often not well-regarded by historians—for example, Herbert Hoover and Jimmy Carter are but two twentieth-century illustrations.

Thus, every president from Reagan to Obama has cast himself as living proof of the American Dream's continued potency. For them, the Dream is not just mouthing words; rather, their personal stories and the moral lessons derived from them are proof that the American Dream— with its emphasis on freedom, equality of opportunity, and individual

---

[2] See "Obama's Admiration of Ronald Reagan," *OpenLeft.com,* January 16, 2008; available at www.openleft.com/showDiary.do?diaryId=3263 (accessed November 16, 2009).

rights—still works. Such "proof" gives political orthodoxy a rigid quality. As historian Daniel Boorstin once asked, "Who would think of using the word 'un-Italian' or 'un-French' as we use the word 'un-American?'" (Boorstin 1953, 14). Political scientist Louis Hartz put it this way: "When one's ultimate values are accepted wherever one turns, the absolute language of self-evidence comes easily enough" (Hartz 1955, 58). Indeed, our advancement of the "American Way of Life" has taken on missionary proportions. In his second inaugural address, for example, George W. Bush argued that the United States had a responsibility to ensure "the expansion of freedom in all the world" (George W. Bush 2005).

But the American Dream and the presidency include much more than mere explication of personal stories. Immigration and the presidency have become intertwined, as immigrants gravitate to presidential candidates who can provide them with the inspiration to pursue their own American Dreams.

Immigrants and the Presidency

For a nation of immigrants, the American Dream has a very special allure. James Truslow Adams captured this appeal in his book *The Epic of America*. In it, he told the story of Mary Antin, a young Russian immigrant, who was found sitting on the steps of the Boston Public Library, writing in a journal:

> This is my latest home, and it invites me to a glad new life. The endless ages have indeed throbbed through my blood, but a new rhythm dances in my veins. My spirit is not tied to the monumental past, any more than my feet were bound to my grandfather's house below the hill. The past was only my cradle, and now it cannot hold me, because I am grown too big; just as the little house in Polotzk, once my home, has now become a toy of memory, as I move about at will in the wide spaces of this splendid palace, whose shadow covers acres. No! It is not I that belong to the past, but the past that belongs to me. America is the youngest of the nations, and inherits all that went before in history. And I am the youngest of America's children, and into my hands is given all her priceless heritage, to the last white star espied through the telescope, to the last great thought of the philosopher. Mine is the whole majestic past, and mine is the shining future. (Adams 1941, 416–417)

Occupying this glorious future has been the objective of every immigrant. Stories like Mary Antin's provide inspiration, of course. But it is the tales of American presidents and would-be presidents who have traveled from humble beginnings to scale the heights of political power that truly endure. The stories of four presidential aspirants are illustrative of the strong association immigrants make between the American Dream and their own aspirations: Alfred E. Smith, John F. Kennedy, Michael S. Dukakis, and Obama.

Alfred E. Smith and the Election of 1928

One of the very first indications of the strong link between the American Dream and the U.S. presidency occurred in 1928, when the Democratic Party selected New York governor Alfred E. Smith to be its standard-bearer. Smith lost in a landslide that year to Republican Herbert Hoover. A seemingly prosperous economy provided a bulwark against any popular rejection of the lock the Republican Party had on the presidency. But the importance of Smith's candidacy to a nation chock-full of immigrants cannot be understated. An exodus of Irish immigrants beginning in the 1840s altered the singularly dominant white Anglo-Saxon Protestant hegemony that characterized the U.S. populace since the nation's inception. This alteration was completed in the years between 1890 and 1924, when the United States experienced a massive migration of immigrants (mostly Catholics and Jews) from eastern, central, and southern Europe. In those years, more than fifteen million people emigrated to the United States (U.S. Department of Commerce 1975, 105–106). These migrants attracted the ire of many. In 1854, Protestant militants destroyed a Catholic church in Boston with gunpowder. Indeed, the established, largely Protestant citizenry bemoaned the creation of "virtual papal states" (White 1983, 8). By the turn of the twentieth century, shopkeepers put so-called NINA signs in their windows, meaning "No Irish Need Apply."

Smith was born on New York City's East Side and was the son of an Irish immigrant. Raised in a poor family, Smith sought employment at the city's famous Fulton Fish Market. When Smith captured the Democratic nomination for president in 1928, it was more than a rags-to-riches story; it signified the acceptance of Catholic immigrants into the highest councils of American life, as the *New Republic* observed: "For the first time a representative of the unpedigreed, foreign-born, city-bred, many-tongued recent arrivals on the American scene has knocked on the door and aspired seriously to the presidency seat in the national council chamber" (Huthmacher 1969, 154). Indeed, Smith's elevation electrified Catholic immigrants. His receptions in heavily Catholic cities, such as Boston, Providence, and Hartford, were overwhelming: 750,000 on the streets in Boston; 100,000 in Hartford; 40,000 in Providence (White 1983, 11). Numbers alone do not reveal the intensity of feeling in the crowds. According to the *Boston Evening Globe,* "No Boston crowd before ever went so mad. No other man ever called up such fervent joyous tumult of emotion from the deep wells of the heart of the city as this best-loved son of American city life" (Huthmacher 1969, 162). Smith himself later wrote of that reception, "So intense was the feeling, so large the throng, that at times I feared for the safety of Mrs. Smith riding with me in the automobile" (Smith 1929, 403).

Although Smith lost the presidency in a landslide, his candidacy put American Catholics foursquare into the Democratic Party, because it had taken a chance to nominate one of their own for the presidency. By doing so, Catholics could derive an important moral lesson from Smith's story—namely, that the American Dream could work for them, too.

John F. Kennedy and the Election of 1960

Smith's defeat did not lessen the American Dream. But it was not the fairy-tale ending Catholics wanted. That came in 1960, when John F. Kennedy became the first Catholic president. When Kennedy was deciding whether to seek the presidency, he had one particularly enthusiastic supporter: his father. Joseph P. Kennedy told his son that being a Roman Catholic would make him a powerful contender:

> Just remember, this country is not a private preserve for Protestants. There's a whole new generation out there and it's filled with the sons and daughters of immigrants from all over the world and those people are going to be mighty proud that one of their own is running for president. And that pride will be your spur, it will give your campaign an intensity we've never seen in public life. Mark my words, it's true. (Barone 1990, 310)

Hearing this, the youthful JFK had only one question left: "Well, Dad, when do we start?" (ibid.). The elder Kennedy's analysis proved correct, and religion became the great divide in the November election. Kennedy won 78 percent of the Catholic vote, while his Republican opponent, Nixon, won 63 percent of the votes cast by white Protestants (ibid., xii).

American Catholics were attracted to Kennedy for several reasons. As late as 1960, most Catholics remained economic "have-nots." Roosevelt's New Deal, which saved many Catholics from economic ruin, was still fresh in their minds. Thanks to Roosevelt, Catholics were beneficiaries of many government programs—especially Social Security—that provided an economic safety net. Moreover, the discrimination that Catholic immigrants were subjected to at the turn of the twentieth century also remained poignant. "No Irish Need Apply" was not just a page in a dusty history book but a sign whose memories still rendered a stigmata of hurt and pain. Nixon wrote in *Six Crises* that, during the 1960 campaign, he "could not dismiss from my mind the persistent thought that, in fact, Kennedy was a member of a minority religion to which the presidency had been denied throughout the history of our nation and that perhaps I, as a Protestant who had never felt the slings of discrimination, could not understand his feelings—that, in short, he had every right to speak out against even possible and potential bigotry" (Nixon 1979, 364). Kennedy tacitly agreed, telling delegates to the Democratic National Convention that his party had taken a "hazardous risk" in choosing him. He reiterated his pledge to uphold the constitution and his oath of office, regardless of any religious pressure or obligation "that might directly or indirectly interfere with my conduct of the presidency in the national interest" (Kennedy 1960).

Still, the existing prejudices against Catholic immigrants were considerable. Newspaper headlines stressed Kennedy's Catholicism: "Democrats Hit Back on Religion" (*New York Times*); "Johnson Blasts 'Haters' Attacks on Catholics" (*Washington Post*); "Creed Issue Must Be Met, Bob Kennedy Says Here" (*Cincinnati Enquirer*); "Mrs. FDR Hits Religious Bias in Talk to Negroes" (*Baltimore Sun*; Nixon 1979, 433–434). For its part, the National Association of Evangelicals sent a distressed letter to pastors, warning: "Public opinion is changing in favor of the church of Rome. We dare not sit idly by—voiceless and voteless" (Goodstein 2004). These headlines reflected and shaped the public's views of the candidates. The morning after the long election night, Nixon's daughter Julie awakened the exhausted candidate to ask, "Daddy, why did people vote against you because of religion?" (Nixon 1979, 465). But it was not a vote against Nixon, per se. Instead, the lesson of the 1960 campaign was that even Catholic immigrants and their heirs could reach the presidency. Aspirations without limits are at the heart of the American Dream.

Michael S. Dukakis and the Election of 1988

In 1988, Democrats once more employed the story of an immigrant-made-good to try to sell their presidential candidate. Massachusetts governor Michael S. Dukakis, the son of Greek immigrants, enveloped his life story into an American Dream mantra. Accepting the 1988 Democratic presidential nomination in its name, Dukakis told the delegates that the American Dream that "carried me to this platform is alive tonight in every part of this country—and it's what the Democratic Party is all about" (Dukakis 1988). Dukakis proclaimed the Democrats to be "America's Party" (Dukakis Praises "America's Party" 1988) and predicted victory "because we are the party that believes in the American Dream" (ibid.).

Dukakis understood how deeply the American Dream was etched into an immigrant's psyche. The immigrant version of it goes something like this: A dispossessed man comes to America after a long journey. He may be overworked but is not oppressed. He may be victimized but is not himself a victim. And the son looks upon the father with pride, while moving several rungs past him on the economic ladder. Dukakis did not deviate from that script. He often spoke of his father's 1912 arrival at Ellis Island, followed by his mother one year later. In his words, they were "poor, unable to speak English, but [had] a burning desire to succeed in their new land of opportunity" (Dukakis 1988). So often did Dukakis advertise his Greek heritage that some of his detractors chortled, "I knew Michael Dukakis before he was Greek." Still, Dukakis continued to tell his story, paying homage to the American Dream at every opportunity:

> My parents came to this country as immigrants, like millions and millions of Americans before them and since, seeking opportunity, seeking the American Dream. They made sure their sons understood that this was the greatest country in the world, that those of us ... who were the sons and daughters of immigrants had a special responsibility to give something back to the country that had opened up its arms to our parents and given so much to them. I believe in the American Dream. I'm a product of it. And I want to help that dream come true for every single citizen in this land, with a good job at good wages, with good schools in every ... community in this country, with

decent and affordable housing that our people can buy and live in, so that we end the shame of homelessness in America, with decent and affordable health care for all working families. . . . The best America is not behind us. The best America is yet to come. (Bush-Dukakis 1988)

That was not to be, for Dukakis lost to George H. W. Bush, garnering just 46 percent of the popular vote and winning only 111 electoral votes. This loss did not mean that the power of the immigrant story was passé. Far from it: In the two decades after Dukakis's ignominious defeat, the number of immigrants entering the United States soared, and the allure of the American Dream—and presidential candidates who embodied it—only intensified.

Barack H. Obama and the Election of 2008

In his book *The Audacity of Hope,* Barack Obama described how today's immigrants are "beneficiaries of a nation more tolerant and more worldly than the one immigrants faced generations ago, a nation that has come to revere its immigrant myth" (Obama 2006, 260). Seeing himself as the son of a migrant who had achieved extraordinary success, Obama sought to convey himself as an exemplar of the American Dream. In a speech to the National Association of Latino Elected and Appointed Officials (NALEO), he declared, "I'm proud to be here today not just as the Democratic nominee for president, but as the first African American nominee of my party, and I'm hoping that somewhere out in this audience sits the person who will become the first Latino nominee of a major party" (Obama 2008a).

Obama's desire to cast himself as the tribune of immigrants was powered by the vastly changing demography of the United States that is transforming a once white Anglo-Saxon Protestant nation into a multiracial, multicultural, and multilingual polity. Consider: When Nixon took the presidential oath in 1969, approximately 9.6 million foreign-born residents lived in the United States. Thirty-two years later, when George W. Bush raised his hand to repeat the same oath, the figure had grown to 28.4 million (Williams 2006, 33). Today, more foreign-born people live in California (8.4 million) than the total population in all of New Jersey, and more foreign-born people are in New York State than the entire population of South Carolina (Buchanan 2002, 2).

In the twenty-first century, two distinct Americas are coming into focus: one, mostly white and English speaking; another, mostly Hispanic and Spanish speaking. In 2006, the Census Bureau reported that Latinos totaled a record 44.3 million (Pew Research Center 2007, 11). For the first time in U.S. history, Latinos outnumber blacks (population 36.7 million) to become the nation's number one minority group (Pew Research Center, 2007, 11). It is estimated that Latinos will account for 60 percent of the U.S. population growth between 2005 and 2050, and the Census Bureau in 2008 issued a bulletin that by 2042 (eight years earlier than anticipated), whites will be the nation's new *minority* (Passel and Cohn 2008, 9; Roberts 2008).

Today, the nation's skin complexion is rapidly changing from white to some form of beige. California, for instance, saw its Anglo population fall by nearly five hundred thousand during the 1990s; as a result, only 46.7 percent of Californians are white, and 32.4 percent are Hispanic (Barone and Cohen 2003, 154). This new demography helped give Obama a solid 2008 victory in the Golden State. Whites constituted just 63 percent of the Californians casting ballots, and they were tepid in their support for Obama, giving him just 52 percent of their votes. But nonwhites made up for Obama's relative lack of support among whites: Blacks constituted 10 percent of the total vote, and they overwhelmingly backed Obama with 95 percent of their votes; Hispanics were 18 percent of the total vote, and they gave Obama 74 percent of their support; Asians composed 6 percent of the votes cast, and 64 percent of them backed Obama; and those of some other race were 3 percent of the vote, and they gave Obama 55 percent of their ballots (Edison Media Research and Mitofsky International 2008). Thanks to such overwhelming nonwhite backing, Obama overwhelmed McCain statewide, 61 percent to 37 percent.

Something similar happened nationally. Although Obama won just 43 percent of white votes cast in 2008, he captured 67 percent of Hispanic support, 62 percent backing from Asians, and 66 percent of the votes cast by other nonwhites. The story of Obama's foreign father, a Kenyan who came to the United States to study on a student visa and married Obama's mother—both college students in Hawaii—only to desert the family later, is well-known. Writing in his autobiography, *Dreams from My Father,* Obama described how his impoverished father, seeking admission to a U.S. college, "yanks the typewriter toward him and begins to type, letter after letter after letter, typing the envelopes, sealing the letter like messages in bottles that will drop through a post office slot into a vast ocean and perhaps allow him to escape the island of his father's shame" (Obama 2004a, 428). And when a letter of acceptance arrived from the University of Hawaii, it became a kind of fulfillment of all that the American Dream offered. As Obama put it, "With the degree, the ascot [tie], the American wife, the car, the words, the figures, the wallet, the proper proportion of tonic to gin, the polish, the panache, the entire thing seamless and natural, without the cobbled-together, haphazard quality of an earlier time—what could stand in his way?" (ibid.).

Obama's story bolstered his standing among immigrants. Consider: In 2004, George W. Bush won 40 to 44 percent of the Hispanic vote, thanks to his standing post–September 11 and his reluctance to engage in discriminatory, anti-immigrant politics. Obama won back some of these Bush supporters precisely because he cast himself as someone who reveled in the "immigrant myth"—namely, that America is a melting pot of many different peoples and yet "is big enough to accommodate all their dreams" (Obama 2006, 269).

Conclusion

As this chapter has demonstrated, the American presidency is not only an office of executive responsibilities; it is a place where the American Dream becomes personified. Americans expect their presidents to do more than pay homage to the American Dream: They want to hear stories of ratification, and they want their presidents to pursue policies that enlarge the scope and the aspirations contained in the idea of the American Dream. As *New York Times* columnist Thomas L. Friedman has so memorably written, "America—with its open, free, no-limits immigrant-friendly society—is still the world's greatest dream machine" (Friedman 2009). Immigrants have expanded our sense of who we as Americans are, and presidents have allowed immigrants (and the rest of us) to dream big.

References

Adams, J. T. 1941. *The epic of America.* Garden City, NY: Blue Ribbon Books.
Alter, J. 2006. *The defining moment: FDR's hundred days and the triumph of hope.* New York: Simon and Schuster.

Barone, M. 1990. *Our country: The shaping of America from Roosevelt to Reagan.* New York: Free Press.

Barone, M., and R. E. Cohen. 2003. *The almanac of American politics, 2004.* Washington, DC: National Journal.

Boorstin, D. J. 1953. *The genius of American politics.* Chicago: University of Chicago Press.

Buchanan, P. J. 2002. *The death of the West: How dying populations and immigrant invasions imperil our country and civilization.* New York: St. Martin's Press.

Burnham, W. D. 1989. The Reagan heritage. In *The election of 1988,* ed. G. M. Pomper, 1–32. Chatham, NJ: Chatham House.

Bush, G.H.W. 1988. Acceptance speech. Republican National Convention, New Orleans, Louisiana, August 18.

Bush, G. W. 2000. Acceptance speech. Republican National Convention, Philadelphia, Pennsylvania, August 4.

———. 2005. Inaugural address. Washington, D.C., January 20.

Bush-Dukakis. 1988. Presidential debate, Winston-Salem, North Carolina, September 25.

Cannon, L. 1991. *President Reagan: The role of a lifetime.* New York: Simon and Schuster.

Clinton, B. 1992. Acceptance speech. Democratic National Convention, New York City, July 16.

Dukakis, M. S. 1988. Acceptance speech. Democratic National Convention, Atlanta, Georgia, July 21.

Dukakis praises "America's Party." 1988. *New York Times,* June 19.

Edison Media Research and Mitofsky International. 2008. California exit poll, November 4.

Flexner, J. T. 1974. *Washington: The indispensable man.* New York: New American Library.

Friedman, T. L. 2009. Advice from Grandma. *New York Times,* November 22.

Goodstein, L. 2004. How the Evangelicals and Catholics joined forces. *New York Times,* May 30.

Hartz, L. 1955. *The liberal tradition in America.* New York: Harcourt Brace Jovanovich.

Huthmacher, J. J. 1969. *Massachusetts: People and politics, 1919–1933.* New York: Atheneum.

Kennedy, J. F. 1960. Acceptance speech. Democratic National Convention, Los Angeles, California, July 15.

Kusnet, D. 1992. *Speaking America: How the Democrats can win in the nineties.* New York: Thunder's Mouth Press.

Luce, H. R. 1941. The American century. *Life,* February 17.

McCain, J. 2008. Concession speech. Phoenix, Arizona, November 5.

Nixon, Richard M. 1960. Acceptance speech. Republican National Convention, Chicago, July 28.

———. 1968. Acceptance speech. Republican National Convention, Miami, August 8.

———. 1979. *Six crises.* New York: Warner Books.

Obama, Barack. 2004a. *Dreams from my father: A story of race and inheritance.* New York: Three Rivers Press.

———. 2004b. Keynote address. Democratic National Convention, Boston, Massachusetts, July 27.

———. 2006. *The audacity of hope: Thoughts on reclaiming the American Dream.* New York: Crown.

———. 2007. Remarks of Senator Barack Obama: Reclaiming the American Dream. Bettendorf, Iowa, November 7.

———. 2008a. Remarks to NALEO. Washington, D.C., June 28.

———. 2008b. Victory speech. Chicago, Illinois, November 5.

———. 2009a. Inaugural address. Washington, D.C., January 20.

———. 2009b. Press conference. Washington, D.C., February 9.

Passel, J. S., and D. Cohn. 2008. *U.S. populations projections, 2005–2050.* Pew Research Center report, February 11.

Pessen, E. 1984. *Log cabin myth: The social backgrounds of presidents.* New Haven: Yale University Press.

Pew Research Center. 2007. *Blacks see growing values gap between poor and middle class.* Press release, November 13.

Plouffe, D. 2009. *The audacity to win: The inside story and lessons of Barack Obama's historic victory.* New York: Viking.

Reagan, R. 1983. Press conference. Washington, D.C., June 28.

Roberts, S. 2008. A generation away, minorities may become the majority in U.S. *New York Times,* August 14.

Roosevelt, F. D. 1933. Inaugural address. Washington, D.C., March 4.

———. 1995. *Fireside chats.* New York: Penguin Books.

Rossiter, C. 1960. *The American presidency.* New York: New American Library.

Sandburg, C. 1954. *Abraham Lincoln, volume three: The war years.* New York: Dell.

Smith, A. E. 1929. *Up to now: An autobiography.* New York: Viking.

Thach, C. C., Jr. 1969. *The creation of the presidency, 1775–1789: A study in constitutional history.* Indianapolis: Liberty Fund.

U.S. Department of Commerce. 1975. *Historical statistics of the United States: Colonial times to 1970.* Washington, DC: Bureau of the Census.

Von Drehle, D. 2009. What would Lincoln do? *Time,* February 16.

White, J. K. 1983. *The fractured electorate: Political parties and social change in southern New England.* Hanover, NH: University Press of New England.

Wicker, T. 1991. *One of us: Richard Nixon and the American Dream.* New York: Random House.

Williams, K. M. 2006. *Mark one or more: Civil rights in multiracial America.* Ann Arbor: University of Michigan Press.

Wirthlin, R. B. 1981. *Final report of the Initial Actions Project.* January 29.

CHAPTER 4

Dreaming in Black and White

James W. Loewen

I N 2007, I asked a class of students in an urban sociology class at a fine Catholic university in the East to fantasize about their futures. Where and how would they be living, fifteen years hence? All but two imagined a life in suburbia, with a spouse, children, grass, and a good job.[1] And that dream was of a *white* suburbia.

To be sure, it was not *all* white. No one objected if, down on their imaginary block, the family of, say, a black health care professional lived.

Nevertheless, a white vision.

Sociologists have long known that people's dreams are limited by their reality. During World War II, researchers asked the public, "What do you want in your postwar house?" and, according to Paul Goodman, "the responses were hopelessly banal." As urban planner Catherine Bauer put it, "People can want only what they know" (Goodman 1962, 5). My students were not imagining a future from scratch. Mostly they were dreaming what they knew, plus about 25 percent. In so doing, these students were not unusual. On the contrary, I had begun class with that fantasy exercise precisely because I knew how it would likely turn out. What students know in the United States—at least what middle- and upper-class whites know throughout most of the country—is residential segregation, especially in the suburbs. And more Americans now live in suburbs than in cities and rural areas combined.

---

[1] The two exceptional students, both of whom imagined life in an urban row house, both came from New York City.

"Hopelessly banal," perhaps, but explicitly racist for certain were the vast subdivisions erected by Levitt and Sons, the largest homebuilder in America after World War II. When the William and Daisy Myers family moved in 1957 into Levittown, Pennsylvania, a "sundown town" that did not allow black residents, white supremacists occupied a nearby house and made it the center of organized opposition. They raised a Confederate flag, played "Dixie" over a loudspeaker at high volume and all hours, and phoned the Myerses with threats. The [White] Citizens' Council circulated this cartoon showing their support for this Northern racism (Kushner 2009, 202, 205; *Exhibit on Levittown* 2002; Citizens' Council 1957, 4). (Reprinted from *The Citizen,* the publication of the Citizens' Council of Mississippi, 1957.)

Life before the Nadir

It was not always this way. A little more than a century ago, Americans lived much more integrated lives, racially and economically. African Americans lived everywhere—in northeast Pennsylvania river valleys, in every Indiana county save one, deep in the north woods of Wisconsin, in every county of Montana and California. Similarly, within cities, African Americans lived everywhere. Reynolds Farley and William Frey (1994, 24), premier researchers on residential segregation, point out that until about 1900, "in northern cities, some blacks shared neighborhoods with poor immigrants from Europe." Even middle-class areas were interracial: "Tiny cadres of highly educated blacks lived among whites in prosperous neighborhoods."

The Index of Dissimilarity ("D") provides a useful measure of the degree of residential segregation in a city or metropolitan area.[2] When D = 0, integration is perfect: Every part of the city has exactly the same racial composition. The number 100 represents complete apartheid: not one black in any white area nor one white in a black area. For values between 0 and 100, D tells the percentage of the smaller group—usually African Americans—that would have to move to whiter areas to achieve a neutral distribution of both races. In 1890, a representative selection of twenty-two Northern cities had an average D of 38—not very segregated. Southern cities were even less segregated spatially, with a D of 22. Most city neighborhoods also contained poor people and rich people—the alley homes in Capitol Hill in Washington, D.C., are an example—partly so the poor could maintain the houses of the rich.[3]

The Nadir of Race Relations

That was life in 1890. Rapid change was already underway. Between 1890 and 1940, racism rose to new heights, and race relations sank to new depths, prompting historians to call this era the "nadir of race relations." Lynchings peaked. Owners expelled black baseball players from the major (and minor) leagues. Unions drove African Americans from such occupations as railroad fireman and meat cutter.

During the nadir, race became embedded in our geography. Whites indulged in race riots that drove blacks out of towns from Oregon to Minnesota to Pennsylvania to Florida, creating sundown towns across the North. Many communities that had no African American residents joined in, passing ordinances that forbade blacks from remaining after dark. Still other towns decided informally not to allow African Americans to settle. Suburbs used zoning and informal policing to keep out black would-be residents and eminent domain to take their property if they did manage to buy some.

---

[2] D is particularly useful, because it is not affected by the overall proportion of African Americans in the metropolitan area, and because it has intuitive clarity. D is calculated for two groups at a time, here blacks and nonblacks.

[3] 1890 averages calculated from Cutler, Glaeser, and Vigdor 2007; cf. Farley and Frey 1994.

In 1914, Villa Grove, near Champaign, Illinois, put up this water tower. Sometime thereafter, the town mounted a whistle on it that sounded at 6 P.M. to warn African Americans to get beyond the city limits. It sounded until about 1998, when it was stopped owing to complaints by neighbors about the noise. Although ordinances are hard to find, this siren embodies one, because putting it up and sounding it required formal action by city hall. Since Villa Grove is on no main route and near no major black population center, its siren also exemplifies an irrational American nightmare. (Photograph by James W. Loewen.)

The nadir took place for a complex of causes. Maybe the antiracist ideology of the Reconstruction era could not have lasted past 1890, having derived in large part from the social events and intellectual developments of the Civil War. Certainly the ideology of imperialism, wafting into the United States on winds from England and Europe, played an important role. So did our continuing Indian wars, culminating in the 1890 massacre at Wounded Knee that sent Native Americans into a nadir of their own. Beginning around 1885, white workers in Wyoming, California, and across the West drove Chinese American workers from whole counties and entire occupations. The rise of eugenics as a "science" was hardly ·coincidental. Perhaps most important was our national acquiescence, also beginning in 1890, as Mississippi passed its new state constitution removing African Americans from citizenship. Since the United States did nothing, all other Southern states and states as distant as Oklahoma followed suit by 1907.

CHRISTOPHER COLUMBUS
BORN IN GENOA, ITALY 1451. DISCOVERED
AMERICA OCTOBER 12, 1492. THIS LAND
OF OPPORTUNITY AND FREEDOM WAS
THUS PRESERVED FOR HUMANITY BY THE
PERENNIAL GENIUS ABIDING IN THE
ITALIAN RACE.

REFURBISHED BY
KNIGHTS OF COLUMBUS 1956

Audiences cackle at the last line on this bust of Christopher Columbus. They "know" Italians are not a race. Italian Americans believed differently in 1920 when they erected this monument at the Indiana State Capitol. By the end of the nadir, however, Italians, Slavs, and other "races" had become one race—"white." Jews, Armenians, and Turks took just a little longer. Without these additions, "whites" would have been outnumbered long ago. Perhaps for the same reason, now the white American Dream seems to be opening to Latinos and Asian Americans. (Photograph by James W. Loewen.)

During the nadir, Mena, the county seat of Polk County, Arkansas, competed for white residents and tourists by advertising what they had—cool summers, pretty homes, and so forth—and the problems they did *not* have. The sentiment hardly died out in 1940. A 1980 article, "The Real Polk County," began, "It is not an uncommon experience in Polk County to hear a new-comer remark that he chose to move here because of 'low taxes and no niggers'" (The Real Polk County 1980).

EVER HEARD OF MENA

THE CITY OF THE OZARK MOUNTAINS
ELEVATION 1200 FEET

Cool Summers	No Mosquitoes
Mild Winters	No Blizzards
Pure Soft Water	No Malaria
Beautiful Scenery	No Drouth
Pretty Homes	No Negroes

Schools and Churches
Lodges and Societies
Parks and Driveways
Fruits and Flowers
Health and Happiness

Telephones, Electric Lights, Water Works, Sewers, Concrete Side-walks, Public Library, all Surrounded by Country Filled With Happy, Healthy, Prosperous People

ADDRESS
SECRETARY MENA COMMERCIAL CLUB
MENA, ARKANSAS

How were we to understand such acts?[4] The easiest way would be to declare that African Americans had never deserved equal rights in the first place. After all, went this line of thought, slavery was over. Now a new generation of African Americans had come of age, never tainted by the "peculiar institution." Why were they still at the bottom? African Americans themselves must be to blame. *They* must not work hard enough, think as well, or have as much drive compared to whites. And if they are the problem, why let that problem near us?[5]

---

[4] "Cognitive dissonance" as developed by Festinger 1957 can help.

[5] The theme of African Americans as the problem does not stand up to scrutiny. Whites forced African Americans from major league baseball not because they could not play well but because they could. Whites expelled black jockeys from the Kentucky Derby not because they were incompetent but because they won fifteen of the first twenty-eight der-bies. They drove blacks out of the job of postal carrier so they could do it themselves, not

So, we did not. In Illinois, the state where I did the most fieldwork, I identified 504 communities that were demographically likely to have been sundown towns. Of these, I got information about the racial policy, formal or informal, of 220. Of those 220, I confirmed 219 as sundown towns. If the same ratio held among towns whose racial policies are unknown, then about 282 of them would be sundown towns, for a total of 501 (Loewen 2005). Statistically, at least 488 had to be sundown towns. (For details of the calculations, see the appendix.) This is about 70 percent of all incorporated municipalities in the state. Similar ratios were found in Oregon, Indiana, and probably several other Northern states. Sundown suburbs were even more common: Across the United States, I estimate that 80 percent of all suburbs kept out black residents.

Large cities did not go sundown, of course, although Tulsa tried, but most of their neighborhoods did. By 1920, the Index of Dissimilarity of the average Northern city had risen from 38 in 1890 to more than 80. By 1940, the South was catching up: Northern cities averaged 89.2, Southern cities 81.0. By 1960, the average Northern city held at 85.6, while D in the average Southern city had risen to an astonishing 91.9.[6]

Suburban Dreams and Nightmares

Unfortunately, coinciding with this increasing racism in American culture came a new ideological drive toward suburbia. The two grew fatally entwined. New technology—streetcars and, soon to come, autos—was sparking new dreams. No longer did maids and handymen have to live nearby, so the new residential dream could be quite different from the status quo. It resurrected elements of the English country home, watered down, as described in sometimes stinging phrases by social

---

because blacks could not do it right. The foregoing seems obvious, but when it comes to housing, even today, deep inside white culture as a legacy from the nadir is the sneaking suspicion that African Americans *are* a problem, so it *is* best to keep them out.

[6] In fact, segregation was even worse than that, especially in the North. At any given moment, Northern metropolitan areas looked more integrated than they really were, owing to the Great Migration, which continued at least to 1968. This influx of African Americans from the South led to blockbusting, in turn creating transitional neighborhoods that were temporarily desegregated and artificially reduced D. After factoring out changing neighborhoods, Ds in both regions would rise, reflecting black movement to the cities, but especially in the North. Perhaps 94 would be a reasonable estimate for the average D in both regions, controlling for transitional neighborhoods. Cf. Taeuber 1965, Taeuber 1982, and Farley and Frey 1994.

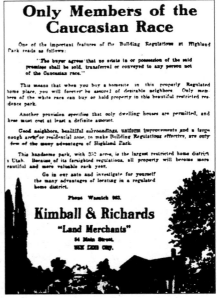

These ads for a residential subdivision at the edge of Salt Lake City show the unfolding of suburban ideology over time. At the left, in 1914, Highland Park advertises pure air; five years later, in 1919, the purity is racial. Possibly the developers were not antiblack personally but merely believed that their new appeal would sell houses faster.

commentators from Thorstein Veblen in 1899 (*The Theory of the Leisure Class*) to Robert Fogelson in 2005 (*Bourgeois Nightmares*).[7]

Fogelson stresses that the new dream community was defined more by what it was *not*—the city, with its noise and odors and, worst of all, all its people—than by what it was. Restrictive covenants abounded. Edina, the most prestigious suburb of Minneapolis/St. Paul, prohibited "fuel storage tanks above ground" and forbade the planting of "shedding poplars, box elders, or other objectionable trees or shrubs." Most importantly:

> No lot shall ever be sold, conveyed, leased, or rented to any person other than one of the white or Caucasian race, nor shall any lot ever be used or occupied by any person other than one of the

---

[7] Cf. Jackson 1985, Baumgartner 1988, et al.

white or Caucasian race, except such as may be serving as
domestics for the owner or tenant of said lot, while said owner
or tenant is residing thereon.

Interestingly, all the Edina restrictions expired in a few decades "except
those in paragraph 8 (racial exclusion)." Those were forever.[8] Thus,
above all, the new American Dream was white.[9]

Ironically, the worse race relations got, the more whites blamed
blacks for the situation. Such occupations as cutting white hair disappeared as black jobs. Washers and dryers replaced black launderers, and
gas heat eliminated interaction with black coal men. Black neighbors
had already disappeared. The lack of contact resulting from this increasing segregation and exclusion allowed whites to demonize African
Americans and their segregated enclaves. People living the white dream
came to fear the black nightmare. Anti-Semitism rose, too, even among
people who had never met a Jew . . . *especially* among people who had
never met a Jew. To this day, public opinion polls show that many non-
black Americans—especially those who live in towns that have few
African Americans whom they might get to know as individuals—still
believe negative generalizations about blacks, at least when these are
phrased politely.

Residential Segregation's Impact on the American Dream, Black and White

As blacks and whites moved away from each other physically, they also
diverged socially and even linguistically. Immigrant children from Ireland or Russia, living among other white children, learned to speak
"white," while African Americans developed increasingly different
accents and created distinctive vocabulary.[10] The separation also took a
toll on black morale. As historians Arna Bontemps and Jack Conroy
observed about Watts, the African American ghetto that exploded into
violence in Los Angeles in 1965: "A crushing weight fell on the spirit of
the neighborhood when it learned that it was hemmed in, that prejudice
and malice had thrown a wall around it" (Bontemps and Conroy 1966, 9).

---

[8] In 1968, a Supreme Court decision and new federal law finally made these restrictions
nonenforceable.

[9] Covenant supplied by Joyce Repya, associate planner for Edina, September 1999.

[10] This is one reason why blacks score much lower than whites, on average, on the SAT.

Children in Detroit live within sight of this playground in Grosse Pointe and know that its bars are aimed at them or were until recently. Only since about 1995 have African Americans been able to live without difficulty in most of the five communities known collectively as Grosse Pointe. (Photograph by James W. Loewen.)

Residents knew it was their *race* that was the problem, so they could not work their way up and out of their predicament. As late as 2002, Leonard Steinhorn could still observe, "An Hispanic or Asian with a third grade education is more likely to live among whites than a black with a Ph.D." (Steinhorn 2002).

In turn, residential segregation made it more likely that African Americans would receive inferior educations, health care, and other public services. Worse yet, confining most African Americans to the opposite of the suburban dream—majority-black inner-city ghettoes—restricted their access to cultural capital, "those learned patterns of mutual trust, insider knowledge about how things really work, encounter rituals, and social sensibilities that constitute the language of power and success."[11] As a result, many young African Americans concluded that reaching the American Dream by the usual (white) methods excluded them. Instead, they turned to less realistic means of achieving it, such as crime or winning the lottery (Samuel 2002; Schultze 1995; Harper's Index 1999).

Our segregated landscape affects white dreams, too. Independent sundown towns, such as Pana, Illinois, or Medford, Oregon, limit the aspirations of children who come of age within them. It is an axiom of American small-town life that "youth goes elsewhere to become somebody," but young people in sundown towns typically hold ambivalent feelings toward the outside world. They are very aware that it differs from their circumscribed little world; indeed, like their parents, high school and college students from all-white towns and suburbs exaggerate the differences and routinely estimate that the population of the United States is 20 to 50 percent black.[12] So they are wary of the outside world and not sure they want to venture out there. "Basically, they didn't go anywhere," a woman from Anna, a sundown town in southern Illinois, said about her friends from Anna-Jonesboro High School. Some Anna residents refuse to go even to nearby Carbondale—it's too black. (Carbondale is 23 percent black.)

Adolescent dreams in elite suburbs display no such limits. These young people have grown up with a sense of entitlement. The world is their oyster, and they intend to harvest its pearls. Their parents mostly do not work in town but in corporate headquarters in the central city or suburban office parks. Their jobs take them across the country, and their frequent-flier miles take their families for vacations around the world. Parochial they are not. And yet, people in the white dream fear the black nightmare: "When we rode the subway," said a former resident of Darien, Connecticut, about his high school friends, "they would ride wide-eyed, thinking they'd be mugged at any moment." Paradoxically, while thus believing that race relations are unrealistically bad, segregated whites

---

[11] Quoting sociologist Orlando Patterson (1997, 9, 20).
[12] The correct figure is about 12 percent.

also think they are unrealistically good. A 2001 poll showed that whites living in overwhelmingly white communities perceived the least discrimination against blacks, while whites in majority black neighborhoods perceived the most (Welch et al. 2001, 85–92).

Where whites live not only affects how they think about blacks—and vice versa—it also influences how they vote. At the beginning of the nadir, Republicans pulled back from their commitment to equal rights to all, regardless of race. Indeed, that retraction was a key reason for the nadir. From William McKinley to Richard Nixon, African Americans could not tell which of the two main parties better served their interests. From time to time, they tried to make common cause with one party or the other, only to find their regard unrequited. Then in 1964 came a sea change. Campaigning for president, Barry Goldwater emphasized that he had opposed the Civil Rights Act of that year. His supporters urged, "Let's make the White House the *white* house again!" Goldwater carried only the Deep South and his home state of Arizona, but his ideological fellow travelers captured the Republican Party, and it has not been the same since. In 1968, Nixon devised his "Southern strategy"—coded references to "states' rights" to imply opposition to using the federal government to overturn the status quo in race relations—to head off George Wallace, a third-party candidate openly hostile to black rights and aspirations. The strategy was misnamed, however. Wallace's popularity was hardly limited to Alabama and Mississippi; he won from a third of to more than half the white vote in such states as Wisconsin and Michigan. Nixon's strategy worked so well, not only in the South but also in sundown towns and white suburbs everywhere, that it has since become bedrock Republican policy (Edsall and Edsall 1992).

The Nightmare Persists Even in the Obama Age

The situation grew still worse. In the words of economist Wilhelmina Leigh: "Between 1950 and 1990 the number of blacks living in all-black census tracts increased from 3 out of 10 to 5 out of 10. At the same time, the number of blacks living in mixed neighborhoods . . . (25% black or less) declined from 25% to 16%" (Leigh 1992, 19). The power of the line—the border between central city and sundown suburb—astounds to this day. Driving west on Eight Mile, the road that forms the northern border of Detroit, houses on the left look like those on the right, but 75 percent of the residents on the left are African American, compared to fewer than 1 percent on the right. Depending on one's social class, the tidy homes and well-kempt lawns of suburban Warren or the McMansions of Grosse Pointe embody many American Dreams. The tidy homes and well-kempt lawns of northern Detroit do not.

Well, they do embody African American dreams, at least in the black working class. Having been excluded from the suburban home-buying boom that marked the United States after World War II, African Americans have struggled to pursue the American Dream—home-ownership in a nice neighborhood—more recently. Always, they have to know, and do know, that whites by definition give lower status to black neighborhoods, precisely because blacks live in them. The election of America's first black president in 2008 was a giant step toward a more integrated nation, to be sure, and Americans saw it that way. Polled a year after Obama's election, 60 percent of all Americans believed that race relations would improve as a result of his presidency, and more than 50 percent of African Americans thought this improvement had already happened just as a result of his election. As Fredrick Harris, who directs the Center on African American Politics and Society at Columbia University, put it, "[E]very time Barack Obama or Michelle Obama and their children are in the press, in the news, this is still a source of pride and a daily reminder that there's been some transformation" (One Year Later 2009).

Unfortunately, the transformation is hardly complete. Obama won the presidency with just over 40 percent of the votes of white males and only 10 percent of the votes of white males in the Deep South. Moreover, despite Obama's triumph, racism is not an aberration in our society but a central part of it. It does not result from bigots but is part of how we do business and is built in—especially to where we live. As African American families try to pursue the American Dream, they still face special obstacles. During the summer of 2009, it became clear why the subprime mortgage loan crisis hit African Americans especially hard. "We just went right after them," said Beth Jacobson, self-described as the top-producing subprime loan officer at the huge Wells Fargo Bank. Wells Fargo "specifically targeted black churches, because it figured church leaders had a lot of influence and could convince congregants to take out subprime loans." Other banks participated. In New York City, for example, black households were "nearly five times as likely to hold high-interest subprime mortgages as whites of similar or even lower incomes," according to the *New York Times* (Powell 2009). Thus, the

American Dreams of many families—especially black families—turned to nightmares.

For a century, the American suburban dream has resulted from and exemplified the conflation of whiteness and prestige. Kenilworth, on Lake Michigan north of Evanston, is the most expensive suburb of Chicago. It is also the whitest. Money does not drive the separation; in Chicago live plenty of black families wealthy enough to afford Kenilworth. Rather, its developer, Joseph Sears, built into its founding ordinances "sales to *Caucasians only*," initially interpreted to bar Jews as well as African Americans. In 1964, a black family finally moved into Kenilworth. Teenagers burned a cross on their lawn, but they stuck it out for twelve years, making some friends in the community. In 2002, however, not one black family lived in Kenilworth (Kilner 1990, 138, 143, emphasis original; *U.S. Census of Population 2000* 2002; Kenilworth realtor 2002). Of course, Kenilworth is a synecdoche for prestigious neighborhoods across America that remain pridefully exclusive, such as Tuxedo Park, probably the wealthiest suburb of New York City; Edina, Minnesota; or, Chevy Chase, Maryland, adjoining Washington, D.C.

The status of all these former sundown suburbs still derives in part from their overwhelmingly white populations. As they become ever more successful, white families in integrated working- or middle-class suburbs still move to Kenilworth. They move not because their previous neighborhoods grew too black for them—indeed, not owing to any dissatisfaction with their previous neighborhoods—but because they are supposed to. Like water, money seeks its outlet. The Kenilworths of America are where the very elite are supposed to live, and people usually do what they are supposed to. Indeed, people usually dream what they are supposed to.

A New American Dream?

Let us close by recalling the college students with whom we began—who dreamt of the suburban good life. Like the residents of Kenilworth, they did not see themselves living in white suburbia out of racism but owing to their (hoped-for) success. Nevertheless, their vision *is* racialized, because it is based on what they know. Their choices, if based on that vision, will lead to continued segregation. Their dream furthers our segregated nightmare. They need to dream outside the box.

We now live in two Americas at once. I do not mean a black America and a white America, although, to be sure, those still exist. I mean that we live in an integrated America (on the job, on most college campuses, on *American Idol,* in the armed forces, in the White House, and in the Catholic Church), and we live in a segregated America (where we live and, too often, how we vote). About race, many of us are white supremacists yet at the same time yearn to transcend white supremacy.

We have two dreams available to us at once. We have Kenilworth as dream, but also Kenilworth as nightmare. When acquaintances announce they are moving to the Kenilworths of America, we need to respond with concern: "Oh no! You're not raising children there, are you?" To change our American Dream, we must stop conflating whiteness and prestige, and responding with dismay to what seems like innocent upward mobility is a good start.

We need a new dream. We are on the cusp of a new dream. In a way, in the 1990s, Michael Jordan represented that new dream—but despite his astonishing popularity across racial lines, white America did not take him home, except as a poster for the teenage son's bedroom. Colin Powell might have represented the new dream—but he never ran for office and instead ran afoul of foul machinations in the George W. Bush administration. Obama does represent the new dream. Can Republicans offer the new dream? Only if they move beyond their Southern strategy and abandon being the party of white supremacy.

Ultimately, to change our American Dream, we must change our racial geography. Toward this end, the recent history of sundown towns offers some hope. Since the middle of the 1990s, many sundown towns and suburbs have given up their policies and integrated peacefully—and not just with Jews, Asian Americans, and Latinos but also with African Americans. Is it too much to believe that we might *un*racialize our dream of the good life in America?

Well, we can dream, can we not?

After all, this is America.

Appendix

Inferential statistics allows us to calculate a range within which we can be confident the true number of sundown towns will fall. We use "the standard error of the difference of two percentages." To find this statistic, first we calculate the standard error of each percentage separately. Beginning with the 218 towns on which we have information, the formula is:

$$s_{p1} = \sqrt{pq/n}$$

where n = the number of towns for which we have data (220), p = the proportion that were sundown (.995), and q = (1 − p) or .005. This standard error = .005, or 0.5 percent. (Actually, this proportion is known without error, or at least without error caused by sampling. Calculating its standard error would be appropriate if we were using a sample drawn from a larger population—say, all towns in the southern half of the state—but here 218 *is* the population. Some statisticians calculate the standard error anyway, just to be conservative or as a surrogate for other forms of error, such as having gathered incorrect evidence on a given town.)

We also need the standard error of the percentage of sundown towns among the 284 towns for which we have no information. Since we do not know this percentage, we assume just 90 percent will be, lower than the most likely estimate of 99.5 percent. Such a conservative assumption provides a larger than likely standard error that results in a more conservative overall estimate. Using the same formula, we substitute: n = 284, p = .9, and q = .1. This standard error = .018, or about 1.8 percent. We then combine these two standard errors using the formula

$$s_{(p1-p2)} = \sqrt{s^2_{p1} + s^2_{p2}}$$

to find the standard error of the difference of two percentages, which = .0182, or 1.82 percent.

We wish to form a confidence interval around 282.6, our best estimate for the number of sundown towns among the 284 unknowns. The more rigorous interval used by statisticians is the "99 percent limit," which means that 99 times out of 100, it will include the actual number of sundown towns. Statistical tables tell that a range that extends 2.58 standard errors above and below our best estimate will include that actual number 99 percent of the time. 2.58 × .0182 = .047, or 4.7 percent; 4.7 percent of 284 = 13.3 towns. So at least 282.6 − 13.3 = 269 of the unknowns will be sundown. Symmetrically, our estimate for the maximum number of sundown towns likely among the unexamined towns would be 282.6 + 13.3 or 296. Of course, numbers above 284 are impossible. To compensate, we might extend the lower limit downward to take in more of the distribution, since its upper limit is clipped, but this correction is not normally computed, is unlikely to be substantial since most of the distribution will be around 282–284, and is at least partly offset by the conservatively calculated standard error described above. Hence I think it is reasonable to conclude that we can be 99 percent confident 269 to 284 of the 284 unknown towns were sundown towns.

Adding the 219 confirmed sundown towns yields an overall estimate, with a 99 percent level of confidence, that the number of sundown towns among all 502 overwhelmingly white towns in Illinois lies between 488 and 503. Our best single estimate for the number of sundown towns in Illinois is 501.

References

Baumgartner, M. 1988. *The moral order of a suburb.* New York: Oxford University Press.

Bontemps, A., and J. Conroy. 1966. *Anyplace but here.* New York: Hill and Wang.

Citizens' Council. 1957. Levittown, PA. *The Citizen* 3, no. 1: 4.

Cutler, D., E. Glaeser, and J. Vigdor. 2007. *Cutler/Glaeser/Vigdor segregation data.* Available at http://trinity.aas.duke.edu/~jvigdor/segregation/allseg.txt.

Edsall, T., and M. Edsall. 1992. *Chain reaction.* New York: Norton.

Exhibit on Levittown. 2002. Harrisburg: Pennsylvania State Museum.

Farley, R., and W. Frey. 1994. Changes in the segregation of whites from blacks during the 1980s. *American Sociological Review* 59, no. 1: 24.

Festinger, L. 1957. *A theory of cognitive dissonance.* Evanston, IL: Row, Peterson.

Fogelson, R. 2005. *Bourgeois nightmares: Suburbia.* New Haven, CT: Yale University Press.

Goodman, P. 1962. *Utopian essays and practical proposals.* New York: Random House.

Harper's Index. 1999. *Harper's Magazine,* November. Available at http://harpers.org/HarpersIndex1999-11.html#7059817545883540.

Jackson, K. 1985. *Crabgrass frontier.* New York: Oxford University Press.

Kilner, C. 1990. *Joseph Sears and his Kenilworth.* Kenilworth, IL: Kenilworth Historical Society.

Kenilworth realtor. 2002. Interview by author.

Kushner, D. 2009. *Levittown.* New York: Walker.

Leigh, W. 1992. Civil rights legislation and the housing status of black Americans: An overview. In *The housing status of black Americans,* ed. W. Leigh and J. Stewart, 5–28. New Brunswick: Transaction.

Loewen, J. 2006. *Sundown towns.* New York: New Press.

One Year Later: Obama's Impact on Race Relations. 2009. *USA Today,* October 23.

Patterson, O. 1997. *The ordeal of integration.* Washington, DC: Civitas/Counterpoint.

Powell, M. 2009. Bank accused of pushing mortgage deals on blacks. *New York Times,* June 6. Available at http://nytimes.com/2009/06/07/us/07baltimore.html.

The Real Polk County. 1980. Mena, AR: no publication indicated (clipping in collection of author).

Samuel, L. 2002. The poor play more—lotteries. *Chicago Reporter,* October. Available at http://findarticles.com/p/articles/mi_m0JAS/is_9_31/ai_93451530.

Schultze, S. 1995. Study shows blacks outspend whites in lottery. *Milwaukee Journal.* Available at http://findarticles.com/p/articles/mi_qn4207/is_19950405/ai_n10191787.

Steinhorn, L. 2002. Is America integrated? *History News Network,* December 23. Available at http://hnn.us/articles/1174.html.

Taeuber, K. 1965. *Negroes in cities.* Chicago, IL: Aldine.

———. 1982. Research issues concerning trends in residential segregation. Madison: University of Wisconsin Center for Demography and Ecology, Working Paper 83-13.

U.S. Census of Population 2000. 2002. Washington, DC: U.S. Census Bureau. Available at http://factfinder.census.gov/servlet/DTTable?_bm=y&-context=dt&-ds_name=DEC_2000_SF1_U&-mt_name=DEC_2000_SF1_U_P016B&-CONTEXT=dt&-tree_id=4001&-all_geo_types=N&-geo_id=16000US1739519&-search_results=16000US1739519&-format=&-_lang=en.

Veblen, T. 1899. *The theory of the leisure class.* New York: New American Library, 1953.

Welch, S., L. Sigelman, T. Bledsoe, and M. Combs. 2001. *Race and place: Race relations in an American city.* Cambridge: Cambridge University Press.

CHAPTER 5

Whose Dream?

Gender and the American Dream

Sandra L. Hanson

T HE AMERICAN DREAM has been a dominant theme in U.S. culture from the very beginning. It is an old dream. Although how the Dream is defined has shifted, it is still a major element in our national identity, and it is assumed that the Dream is for all Americans. Alexis de Tocqueville commented on the "charm of anticipated success" in his classic *Democracy in America* (Cullen 2003). The Dream is an enticing one. Cullen 2003 notes the irony that the Dream began with the Puritans who believed in manifest destiny and the notion that they had no control over their successes or failures. It is also ironic that this Dream remained alive through periods of American history when racial apartheid and slavery existed and when large groups of Americans (e.g., women and African Americans) could not vote.

This chapter focuses on gender and the American Dream. A certain mystique is associated with this Dream. The Dream is demystified here in that a potential gender divide in values and opportunities often associated with the American Dream is examined. First, some background on gender and a number of indicators of achievement associated with the American Dream are provided. Additional background on gender and attitudes about inequality and what it takes to get ahead is discussed. A unique series of public opinion polls on the American Dream is then examined to determine the presence and extent of a gender divide in the definition of the Dream and the ability to achieve it. Additionally the chapter considers whether these attitudes about the American Dream and current opinions on the economy and President Barack Obama have changed over time. Zogby International conducted these surveys beginning in 1998. The most recent surveys are from 2009.

Background

The American Dream in the Twenty-first Century

Jim Cullen (2003) and others (Ho 2007; Johnson 2006; Moen and Roeh-ling 2005; Newman 1993; Shapiro 2004; Sherraden 1991) have suggested that the American Dream and this "glue" that binds us together may be unraveling, as we see a growing wealth gap, ongoing race inequality, an expanding poor immigrant population, and continued sexism in all aspects of American life. Perhaps the twenty-first century is not a time of increasing progress toward the American Dream.

The definition of the American Dream is multifaceted. Does the Dream refer to wealth, religious freedom, freedom of expression, political reform, educational attainment, or access to housing and health care? In the end, historically and today, the Dream is all these things, but it is especially about wealth (Garfinkle 2006). It is about money. In the United States, status (wealth) is believed to be achieved, not ascribed. It is presumed that those who do not achieve are less worthy and work less hard. Thus, inequality is justified, and the Dream can stay alive in the context of one of the wealthiest nations with one of the greatest wealth divides. Cullen 2003 suggests that this loyalty to a Dream that does not exist is a blind loyalty. The next section briefly examines a number of indicators of gender equality in areas of life associated with the American Dream involving education, income, occupations, politics, and opportunity.

The Reality: The Gender Divide

Education. Women and girls have made considerable gains in the U.S. education system in the past century (AAUW 2008). However, gendered education systems, gender tracking, and the hidden curriculum continue to result in equally confidant and intelligent boys and girls leaving adolescence with two different outcomes. Boys experience gains in self-esteem and standardized test scores (especially in science), and girls experience losses in both of these areas (AAUW 2008; Osborne 2001; Prettyman 1998). Although young girls do not start out with low achievement in science, early in the high school years, many girls experience the beginning of a departure from science areas typified by enrollment in fewer science courses, lowered achievement, and increasingly negative attitudes (Hanson 2009; NSF 2008). This "chilling out" occurs even for young women who have shown promise and talent in science.

Today women attend college and graduate from college at a higher rate than men, but they enter majors that assure them of positions in lower-status, lower-paid female-dominated occupations (Lindsey 2005). Almost half of women who enter college with science-related interests switch to other majors (ibid.). Some research has suggested that women in single-sex schools have higher levels of aspirations, self-confidence, leadership qualities, independence, and interest (and performance) in math and the sciences than those in co-ed schools (Riordan 2002).

Most schools have not achieved gender equity in educational resources (whether in sport or in other areas) as mandated by Title IX (National Coalition for Women and Girls in Education 2008; Women's Sports Foundation 1997, 2002). Partisan politics, backlash, inconsistent court rulings, and erroneous media accounts about quotas have worked against Title IX enforcement (Lindsey 2005).

Earnings. In 1961, working women earned fifty-nine cents to a man's dollar. Today, working women average seventy-seven cents to a man's dollar (Institute for Women's Public Policy Research 2007). This represents progress. Yet the trend involves the income gap's closing by just fifteen percentage points in the past few decades. At this rate, it will be 2057 before we close the gender gap in wages (Institute for Women's Public Policy Research 2007; National Committee on Pay Equity 2009). Enforcement of the Equal Pay Act and Title VII of the Civil Rights Act (prohibiting unequal pay for similar work by men and women) remains low, and it is extremely difficult to prove wage discrimination in the U.S. court system (Frey, Gresch, and Yeasting 2001; National Committee on Pay Equity 2009).

Occupations. Women work in different sectors of the labor force than men. The U.S. labor force is gender stratified. Those occupations typically held by women provide lower wages than jobs staffed primarily by men. When firms have employees that are 76 to 90 percent male, wages are 40 percent higher than similar firms employing women (Frey, Gresch, and Yeasting 2001). About three-fourths of women workers have experienced sexual harassment in the workplace (Lindsey 2005). Only 4.5 percent of corporate officers in Fortune 500 companies are women, up from 4.3 percent a decade ago. The Feminist Research Center (2000) reports that at this rate, it will be 2116 before parity is achieved.

Politics. The U.S. Constitution does not have an Equal Rights Amendment. In 2009, women held 17 percent of the seats in the 111th Congress. The average female representation in parliaments (worldwide) is 18.6 percent (Inter-Parliamentary Union 2009). Seventy-one nations have a greater percentage of female (national) legislators than does the United States (Wallechinsky 2007). The United States has never had a woman president, yet nations that are more traditional and socially conservative regarding women have elected women to their highest public offices. Women have served as presidents or prime ministers of countries as diverse as Ireland, Britain, Germany, Norway, Finland, Iceland, Latvia, Malta, the Philippines, Indonesia, Pakistan, Israel, Sri Lanka, Liberia, Turkey, Georgia, Serbia, Dominica, Chile, Bolivia, Portugal, and Argentina (for a complete listing, see Lewis 2007).

Overlap in Inequality by Gender, Race, and Class. Some of the poorest and the least able to achieve the Dream in the United States are poor women of color (National Center for Poverty 2009). Although 13 percent of women are poor, this figure is 9 percent for white women, and nearly triple that (25 percent) for black women (McKinnon 2003). This high rate of poverty has implications for children. Among black children living with their mothers (but not their fathers), 50 percent are living in poverty (Childstats.gov 2008). Census data show that since 1980, more black children live in one-parent families than in two-parent families (Joint Center Data Bank 2007).

Opportunity. Inequality exists in gender opportunity, not just in gender outcomes in the United States. That is, gaining the Dream is not based on qualifications alone. Those who have achieved more education, income, better occupations, and access to homes and health care are not necessarily more qualified. For example, research shows that men are paid more for what they do largely because they are men (Murphy and Graff 2009). A woman needs an extra degree to receive the same earnings as a man (Institute for Women's Policy Research 2007).

Background on Attitudes about Inequality: Who Sees the Cracks in the Dream?

United States vs. Other Countries. Lipset 1996 argues that American culture is exceptional. Part of this uniqueness is bound up with the

American Dream. Research on attitudes about getting ahead in the United States and elsewhere (Hanson, Kennelly, and Fuchs 2007; Kluegel and Smith 1986; Mason and Kluegel 2000) shows that Americans tend to see individual hard work and effort as key to getting ahead. That is, anyone can make it if they just try hard enough. In opinion surveys from other countries, it is more common to see attitudes that acknowledge the roles of such structures as race, gender, and class in affecting opportunities and privilege in who gets ahead. Attitude surveys from other countries show much more support for the notion that working hard sometimes is not enough.

Women vs. Men. Social scientists have consistently shown that women are more likely than men to acknowledge that all do not have equal opportunity. They are more likely to acknowledge racism, sexism, and other factors that limit the ability to achieve the Dream. This acknowledgment could be because women have experienced inequality and, as relative outsiders, can better see the cracks in the Dream (Kane 2000). It could be that gendered socialization has encouraged more "other-directed" thinking among women (Beutel and Marini 1995). It also could be (as Carol Gilligan's [1982] classic work suggests) that gendered socialization has resulted in a moral code among women that stresses social justice (a morality of caring) more than the more rational bases of morality among men.

Our brief review of indicators of inequality and beliefs about inequality shows considerable gender variation in some of the indicators and core principles associated with the American Dream. We turn now to an examination of the Zogby data measuring public opinion on the American Dream.

Methods

Data

Zogby International Polling has been collecting survey data on the American Dream since 1998.[1] In these surveys, respondents are asked about such issues as what the American Dream is, what affects it, and whether they will be able to achieve it. Zogby International survey questions on

---

[1] See the Methods Appendix for more detail on the sampling and interview protocol for the Zogby surveys.

the economy and President Obama are also considered here. The analyses begin with a number of questions from the 2001 survey year, since it included the largest number of American Dream questions. In 2001, 3,020 adults were included in the sample. Survey data from 1998 (N = 1,515), 1999 (N = 1,691), 2004 (N = 985), 2005 (N = 14,467), 2007 (N = 4,009), 2008 (N = 8,100), and 2009 (January: N = 3,498; May: N = 4,037; June; N = 4,436; and September: N = 4,144) are also examined.

Samples for the 1998–2004 and 2007–2009 surveys were randomly drawn from nationally listed telephones. Zogby International surveys employ sampling strategies in which selection probabilities are proportional to population size within area codes and exchanges. Up to six calls are made to reach a sampled phone number. Cooperation rates are calculated using one of the American Association for Public Opinion Research's (AAPOR's) approved methodologies[2] and are comparable to other professional public-opinion surveys conducted using similar sampling strategies.[3] Cooperation rates were calculated by adding completed and incomplete interviews and dividing this by the sum of the completed, incomplete, and refused interviews. Rates for 1998, 1999, 2001, 2004, 2007, 2008, January 2009, May 2009, July 2009, and September 2009 are (respectively) 24 percent, 22 percent, 16 percent, 18 percent, 12.6 percent, 15.7 percent, 12.8 percent, 11.9 percent, 10.9 percent, and 10.9 percent. Weighting by region, party, age, race, religion, and gender is used to adjust for nonresponse. The margins of error for 1998, 1999, 2001, 2004, 2007, 2008, January 2009, May 2009, July 2009, and September 2009 are (respectively) ± 2.5, 2.4, 1.9, 3.2, 1.6, 1.1, 1.6, 1.6, 1.5, and 1.5. Margins of error are higher in subgroups.

Surveys were conducted by telephone in all years except 2005. In 2005, a sampling of Zogby International's online panel, which is representative of the adult population of the United States, was invited to participate in a Web survey. Weights were added (region, party, age, race, gender) to more accurately reflect the population. Panel respondents were e-mailed invitations to participate in the survey, and 59 percent agreed to participate. The margin of error in the 2005 survey is ±.8.[4]

---

[2] See COOP4 (p. 38) in *Standard Definitions: Final Dispositions of Case Codes and Outcome Rates of Surveys* (Deerfield, IL: American Association for Public Opinion Research, 2000).

[3] Jane M. Sheppard and Shelly Haas, *Cooperation Tracking Study: April 2003 Update* (Cincinnati, OH: Council for Marketing and Opinion Research, 2003).

[4] The low margin of error here is a result of taking a random sample of a large representative sampling of Americans with e-mail addresses.

Measures

Definition of the American Dream. Three questions are examined that focus on the definition of the American Dream. The first asks whether the respondent and his or her family consider the American Dream to be mainly about achieving material goods or about spiritual happiness. The second asks about goals in life and provides a number of categories of response, including material success, spiritual fulfillment, and not being able to achieve the Dream. The third question asks whether the respondent's idea of the American Dream has changed over the years.

Is the American Dream Achievable? Seven survey questions address the issue of whether the respondent thinks that it is possible (for self or family) to achieve the American Dream. These questions asked the respondent to agree or disagree with statements on whether it is possible for the respondent and his or her family to achieve the dream (or perhaps it does not exist); confidence that one's children will have a better life than the respondent; whether most middle-class Americans can achieve the American Dream; whether overall equality of opportunity exists in achieving the Dream; whether lack of material success has forced changes in priorities; whether material wealth has brought fulfillment; and whether one aspect of the Dream—a larger home—is possible.

What Affects One's Ability to Achieve the Dream? Two survey items inquired about factors associated with the Dream. Respondents are asked how significant the government has been in helping them achieve the Dream and whether one political party or the other has been more effective in helping Americans achieve the Dream.

Other. A number of other items (from 2009 Zogby surveys) related to the economy and President Obama are also examined. Questions on the economy inquire about the respondent's expectations (regarding his or her economic situation) for 2009, evaluation of his or her personal financial situation, and how secure the respondent feels in his or her job. Regarding President Obama, questions inquire about the respondent's confidence in the president's ability to handle the economy, expectations for the economy in the president's first year, attitude toward the president's economic policies (as generational investment or debt), and overall opinion of the president. Exact wording of all survey questions is included in the tables.[5]

Analyses

Given the categorical nature of the study variables and the research questions concerning gender differences in attitudes about the American Dream, we use cross-tables to examine gender differences in responses to the survey questions. Chi-square statistics are used to test for significance. A good number of American Dream items are included in the 2001 American Dream survey. Table 5.1 includes an examination of these items for men and women. Surveys conducted in 2009 also include some items inquiring about the American Dream as well as items on the economy and President Obama. Table 5.2 presents men's and women's responses to the 2009 survey questions. Finally, a number of questions inquiring about the American Dream are included in multiple surveys. Table 5.3 examines the changes over time in men's and women's responses to these survey items.

Findings

Data in Table 5.1 allow an examination of men's and women's attitudes about various aspects of the American Dream using items from the 2001 Zogby survey on the American Dream.

Is There Gender Variation in the Definition of the American Dream?

The first three items in Table 5.1 address the issue of gender variation in the definition of the American Dream. On each, the opinions of men and women differ significantly. Overall, the most consistent gender differences in the 2001 survey involve the *definition* of the Dream more than whether it is *achievable* or what *factors affect* it. In response to the first question about the nature of the American Dream, slightly more men than women (34 percent vs. 30 percent) say it is mainly about achieving material goods. Women are considerably more likely than men to say the Dream is about achieving spiritual happiness (54 percent vs. 48 percent). An interesting finding is that men *and* women are more

---

[5] Sometimes wording is slightly different between similar survey questions across survey years.

TABLE 5.1 Men's and women's attitudes about the American Dream: Zogby 2001 Survey

	Male	Female
WHAT IS THE AMERICAN DREAM?		
1. Do you and your family consider the American Dream to be mainly about achieving material goods, or is it more about finding spiritual happiness?		
a. Material goods	*34%*	*30%*
b. Spiritual happiness	*48*	*54*
c. Not sure	*18*	*16*
N	1,455	1,564
2. Which of the following descriptions best represents your goals in life?		
a. Material success	*27*	*21*
b. Spiritual fulfillment	*49*	*57*
c. American Dream means material success. It exists but is more likely to be attained by my children and not by me.	*11*	*11*
d. I cannot achieve the American Dream	*7*	*7*
e. Not sure	*6*	*5*
N	1,456	1,563
3. Has your idea of the American dream changed in recent years?		
a. Yes	*38*	*44*
b. No	*60*	*54*
c. Not Sure	*2*	*2*
N	1,455	1,564
IS THE AMERICAN DREAM ACHIEVABLE?		
4. Do you feel that it is possible for you and your family to achieve the American Dream, or would you say it does not exist?		
a. Achieve dream	78	75
b. Does not exist	16	18
c. Not sure	7	7
N	1,455	1,565
5. Do you agree or disagree that most middle-class Americans can achieve the American Dream?		
a. Agree	74	72
b. Disagree	21	24
c. Not sure	5	4
N	1,455	1,564

(*continued*)

TABLE 5.1 *Continued*

	Male	Female
6. Is there equal opportunity for all Americans to achieve the American Dream?		
a. Yes	*56*	*50*
b. No	*41*	*47*
c. Not sure	*3*	*4*
N	1,456	1,564

CAN YOU ACHIEVE THE AMERICAN DREAM?		
7. If you have not succeeded in material ways, have you been forced to change your priorities?		
a. Yes	31	30
b. No	63	66
c. Not sure	6	4
N	768	913

8. Have you succeeded in attaining a measure of material wealth but still sense a lack of fulfillment in your life?		
a. Yes	27	25
b. No	70	71
c. Not sure	3	4
N	706	885

9. Please tell me how likely it is that you or someone in your household will acquire any of the following within the next decade—own a larger home?		
a. Very likely	*25*	*21*
b. Somewhat likely	*18*	*18*
c. Somewhat unlikely	*6*	*7*
d. Very unlikely	*16*	*18*
e. Already have	*14*	*12*
f. No interest	*21*	*24*
g. Not sure	*0*	*0*
N	1,455	1,565

likely to say that the Dream is about spiritual happiness rather than achieving material goods in 2001.

On the next item, a significant gender difference is again evident, with more men than women (27 percent vs. 21 percent) saying that their goals in life involve material success. Although men and women are more likely to stress spiritual than material goals in life, women are

TABLE 5.1 *Continued*

	Male	Female
WHAT AFFECTS ONE'S ABILITY TO ACHIEVE THE AMERICAN DREAM?		
10. How significant has the government been in helping you achieve the American Dream?		
a. Very significant	8	8
b. Somewhat significant	23	23
c. Less than significant	21	23
d. Insignificant	46	43
e. Not sure	2	3
N	1,455	1,564
11. Which political party better represents a party that helps Americans achieve the American Dream? (2001)		
a. Democrat	*33*	*37*
b. Republican	*29*	*25*
c. Other	*21*	*14*
d. Not sure	*17*	*24*
N	1,455	1,564

Notes: Values for each response are percentages of individuals selecting that response. Values may not total 100 percent due to rounding. Sample sizes are given for each question. Italic type indicates that the male-female difference is significant at the .05 level (chi-square test).

more likely than men to report spiritual goals. Men and women are equally likely to say that their children (not the respondents) will be more likely to achieve the material aspects of the Dream or that they themselves cannot achieve it.

Finally, the respondents are asked a question about whether their idea of the American Dream had changed in recent years. More women than men (44 percent vs. 38 percent) agree with this statement. However, in 2001, a majority of both men and women believe that their idea of the American Dream has not changed in recent years.

Is There Gender Variation in Whether Respondents Think It Is Possible to Achieve the American Dream?

Men and women are much more in agreement on the 2001 survey items asking about a number of issues involving the possibility of achieving the American Dream. Chi-square statistics reveal significant gender differences on only two of the six survey items. When differences exist, women are less optimistic than men.

Women and men are in agreement on questions asking about them and their families achieving the Dream and the opportunity for most middle-class Americans to achieve the Dream. A large majority feel that it is possible for them and their families to achieve the Dream (at least 75 percent). Almost as many believe that most middle-class Americans can also achieve this Dream. This optimism on the part of women respondents is interesting given the gender divide that we show in indicators of achieving the American Dream.

The question on succeeding in material ways shows that men and women agree that even if they have not succeeded here, they have not changed their priorities (63 percent of men and 66 percent of women). Similarly, male and female respondents agree that if they have achieved material success, they are fulfilled (approximately 70 percent of each).

When asked more specifically about the ability of ALL Americans to achieve the American Dream, women in the survey are significantly less optimistic than men. Fifty percent of women and 56 percent of men answer "yes" to the question about equality of opportunity in achieving the Dream. It is interesting that both male and female respondents in the Zogby 2001 survey are considerably more optimistic about the ability of middle-class Americans to achieve the American Dream than they are for all Americans to achieve this dream.

The final item measuring an aspect of achieving the Dream in 2001 suggests that men and women significantly differ on their opinion regarding the respondent or someone in their household acquiring a major indicator of the Dream—a larger home—within the next decade. Women are less optimistic. It is not a large difference, but 25 percent of men and 21 percent of women think that this achievement is "very likely." More women than men (18 percent vs. 16 percent) consider this to be "very unlikely." Although gender differences are significant, more than a third of both men and women state that it is "very likely" or "somewhat likely" that someone in their families will own a larger home in the next decade.

Is There Gender Variation in the Factors that People Feel Affect Their Abilities to Achieve the American Dream?

Interestingly, no gender differences exist in opinion about the role of government in helping achieve the American Dream in the 2001 survey

(Americans agree that the government plays a small role here). There is a gender difference, however, in opinion on which political party helps Americans achieve the American Dream. A larger percent of women (relative to men) feel that the Democratic Party is more helpful in this regard (37 percent vs. 33 percent). Likewise, a larger percentage of men (relative to women) believe that the Republican Party provides more help to Americans in achieving the Dream. Both men and women, however, are more likely to state that the Democratic Party has done more than the Republican Party to help Americans achieve the Dream.

2009 Survey Items on One's Children Getting Ahead, the Economy, and President Obama

Table 5.2 includes a number of survey items from more recent (2009) Zogby surveys. The first item in the table asks about the respondent's confidence that his or her children will have a better life than the respondent. It was asked before President Obama took office (January 6, 2009) and again several months after he took office (May 21, 2009). Significant (but small) gender differences are displayed in both survey periods, but the nature of the difference shifts. In the earlier survey, men are more optimistic on their children having a better life. In the later survey, women are slightly more optimistic. The large percentage of male and female respondents (almost a third) who respond "not very" to the question about their confidence in their children having a better life is interesting given the optimism that men and women show in the 2001 survey on issues involving respondents (and their families) achieving the Dream.

The next items in Table 5.2 examine gender differences in a number of issues involving the economy and finances. Although the differences are not large, male and female respondents differ significantly on each of these items. Women are slightly less optimistic than men on the first item inquiring about the respondent's economic situation for 2009. Similarly, they are slightly less optimistic when asked to rate their personal financial situations. However, women are somewhat more likely to rate their situations as poor in the survey period before Obama's presidency (January 6, 2009) relative to after President Obama is in office (May 21, 2009). Similarly, the percentage of women who rank their personal financial situations as good increases between the two survey periods (this increase occurs for men as well, with men being more optimistic than women in both survey periods).

TABLE 5.2 Men's and women's attitudes about the American Dream: Zogby 2009 Survey

	1-06-2009		5-21-2009	
	Male	Female	Male	Female
CHILDREN WILL HAVE A BETTER LIFE?				
1. How confident are you that your children will have a better life than you?				
a. Very	16%	12%	10%	13%
b. Fairly	31	31	24	26
c. Not very	29	30	33	30
d. Not at all	13	13	15	12
e. Not sure/No children	12	15	18	19
N	1,634	1,844	1,880	2,119
THE ECONOMY AND FINANCES				
2. In terms of your own economic situation, what are your expectations for 2009?				
a. It will get worse.	19	20		
b. It will stay the same.	50	49		
c. It will get better.	26	22		
d. Not sure	5	9		
N	1,635	1,843		
3. How would you rate your personal financial situation?				
a. Excellent	5	4	5	5
b. Good	33	28	38	34
c. Fair	46	44	43	41
d. Poor	16	23	14	20
e. Not sure	0	1	0	0
N	1,635	1,842	1,879	2,120
4. How secure do you feel in your current job?				
b. Fairly	38	32	38	31
c. Not very	11	11	15	12
d. Not at all	11	11	9	9
e. Not sure	11	16	10	17
N	1,634	1,843	1,880	2,119

TABLE 5.2 *Continued*

	1-06-2009		5-21-2009	
	Male	Female	Male	Female
THE PRESIDENCY—OBAMA				
5. Please tell us your level of confidence for Barack Obama's ability to handle the following issue—the economy.				
a. Very confident	*25*	*34*		
b. Somewhat confident	*29*	*30*		
c. Not very confident	*18*	*15*		
d. Not at all confident	*27*	*19*		
e. Not sure	*2*	*2*		
N	1,635	1,843		
6. In terms of improving the economy, what are your expectations for the first year of the Obama administration?				
a. The economy will continue to decline but at a slower rate.	*53*	*47*		
b. The economy will stay the same.	*26*	*28*		
c. The economy will grow.	*12*	*12*		
d. Not sure	*9*	*13*		
N	1,634	1,844		
7. Do you view President Obama's economic policies as generational investment or debt?				
a. Generational investment	*32*	*43*		
b. Debt	*61*	*45*		
c. Not sure	*7*	*12*		
N	2,085	2,351		
8. What is your opinion of President Barack Obama?				
a. Very favorable			*33*	*39*
b. Somewhat favorable			*13*	*20*
c. Somewhat unfavorable			*12*	*12*
d. Very unfavorable			*42*	*28*
e. Not familiar			*0*	*0*
f. Not sure			*0*	*1*
N			1,880	2,118

Notes: Values for each response are percentages of individuals selecting that response. Values may not total 100 percent due to rounding. Sample sizes are given for each question. Italic type indicates that the male-female difference is significant at the .05 level (chi-square test).

The last of the financial questions presented in Table 5.2 asks about job security. Again, the differences here are small but significant. Although the percentage of men and women replying that they are "very" secure in their current jobs is quite similar, men are more likely to say that they are "fairly" secure (38 percent vs. 32 percent in January 2009). Responses to the job item change little between the first (January 2009) and second (May 2009) surveys.

Finally, results in Table 5.2 show gender differences on opinion about President Obama. Responses to a question about confidence in Obama's ability to handle the economy (measured before Obama took office) show that women respondents are significantly more likely than male respondents to be "very confident" (34 percent vs. 25 percent). Men are more likely than women to report that the economy will continue to decline in the first year of the administration (53 percent vs. 47 percent). When asked whether President Obama's economic policies are generational investment or debt, women are significantly more likely to report "investment" (43 percent vs. 32 percent). Consistent with this trend, the last item in Table 5.2 shows that female respondents are more likely than male respondents to have a "very favorable" view of President Obama (39 percent vs. 33 percent).

Have There Been Changes over Time in Attitudes about the American Dream?

Results presented in Table 5.3 show changes over time in public opinion on five survey questions included in the Zogby polls. The first item in Table 5.3 is "For you and your family, do you consider the American Dream to be mainly about achieving material goods, or is it more about finding spiritual happiness?" In all but one survey year (January 2009), starting in 1998 and ending in May 2009, both men and women are more likely to answer "spiritual happiness" than "material goods." However, results show that men and women increasingly think that the American Dream is about material goods. The January 2009 survey is the first survey in which more respondents (male and female) report "material goods" than "spiritual happiness" in their responses. In May 2009, women are again more likely to report "spiritual happiness" than "material goods," but this is not the case for men. With regard to gender patterns, in each survey year (with the exception of January 2009), women are significantly more likely than men to answer the question about the American Dream with the "spiritual happiness" response. The

TABLE 5.3 Change in men's and women's attitudes on the American Dream: Zogby American Dream Survey

1. For you and your family, do you consider the American Dream to be mainly about achieving material goods, or is it more about finding spiritual happiness?

	1998		1999		2001	
	Male	Female	Male	Female	Male	Female
a. Material goods	26%	17%	25%	17%	34%	30%
b. Spiritual happiness	49	63	50	64	48	54
c. Not sure	25	20	25	19	18	16
N	744	839	812	878	1,453	1,564

	2005		1-06-2009		5-21-2009	
	Male	Female	Male	Female	Male	Female
a. Material goods	39	40	38	38	40	35
b. Spiritual happiness	45	42	36	36	41	44
c. Not sure	16	18	26	26	19	21
N	6,820	7,328	1,635	1,843	1,879	2,118

2. Which of the following descriptions best represents your goals in life?

	2001		2004		2005		2007	
	Male	Female	Male	Female	Male	Female	Male	Female
a. Material success	27	20	34	25	30	25	44	29
b. Spiritual fulfillment	49	57	43	53	39	36	33	38
c. American Dream means material success. It exists, but it is more likely to be attained by my children and not by me.	11	11	8	7	4	5	3	4
d. I cannot achieve the American Dream.	7	7	8	7	14	8	9	14
e. Not sure	6	5	7	8	13	16	10	15
N	1,456	1,563	581	623	6,818	7,328	1,932	2,077

	2008		1-06-2009		5-21-2009		9-25-2009	
	Male	Female	Male	Female	Male	Female	Male	Female
a. Material success	46	34	34	26	29	20	40	28
b. Spiritual fulfillment	40	47	34	32	35	40	31	39
c. American Dream means material success. . . .	4	5	8	5	7	5	6	
d. I cannot achieve the American Dream.	11	15	11	15	14	13	14	14
e. Not sure	—	—	16	19	17	20	11	13
N	3,906	4,194	1,635	1,844	1,880	2,120	1,948	2,196

(continued)

TABLE 5.3 *Continued*

3. Please tell me how likely it is that you or someone in your household will acquire any of the following within the next decade—own a larger home? (2001)						
	1998		1999		2001	
	Male	Female	Male	Female	Male	Female
a. Very likely	17%	11%	18%	12%	25%	21%
b. Somewhat likely	16	13	16	14	18	18
c. Somewhat unlikely	7	5	7	5	6	7
d. Very unlikely	49	62	49	60	16	18
e. Already have	10	8	9	8	14	12
f. No interest	—	—	—	—	21	24
g. Not sure	1	1	1	1	0	0
N	744	841	811	878	1,455	1,565

4. Do you feel that it is possible for you and your family to achieve the American Dream, or would you say it does not exist?								
	2001		2004		1-06-2009		5-21-2009	
	Male	Female	Male	Female	Male	Female	Male	Female
a. Achieve dream	77	75	80	65	60	52	62	55
b. Does not exist	16	18	16	28	20	24	21	26
c. Not sure	7	7	4	7	20	24	17	19
N	1,455	1,565	474	512	1,634	1,844	1,879	2,119

5. Do you agree or disagree that most middle-class Americans can achieve the American Dream?						
	2001		1-06-2009		5-21-2009	
	Male	Female	Male	Female	Male	Female
a. Agree	74	72	58	49	58	49
b. Disagree	21	24	26	30	28	32
c. Not sure	5	4	16	21	14	19
N	1,455	1,564	1,634	1,843	1,878	2,119

Notes: Values for each response are percentages of individuals selecting that response. Values may not total 100 percent due to rounding. Sample sizes are given for each question. Italic type indicates that the male-female difference is significant at the .05 level (chi-square test).

absence of gender difference in responses on the January 2009 survey is part of a larger trend that reveals a diminishing gender gap. In 1998, 26 percent of men and 17 percent of women agree that the Dream is about material goods. These numbers are larger and more similar beginning in 2001 and continue to increase through the 2005 survey year (39 percent of men and 40 percent of women report "material goods" in their responses to the 2005 American Dream question). It is interesting to note that the survey following President Obama's election marks the first and only time that male and female respondents see material goods as more important than spiritual happiness in their responses to this Zogby survey item. In the next (May 2009) survey, the gender gap returns, and women (but not men) again report that spiritual components are more important than material.

When asked about their goals in life, men and women (but especially women) are increasingly unsure what their goals are. These changes in opinion are quite large with, for example, only 5 percent of women being unsure in 2001 and 19 percent being unsure in January 2009. As with the trend in the first survey item in Table 5.3 (regarding definition of the American Dream), the results from this survey item on goals in life suggest that spiritual fulfillment is becoming less a part of the Dream for both men and women. An interesting switch occurs in 2005, when, for the first time, men are more likely to say that spiritual fulfillment is a goal.

Results for the third item in Table 5.3 show that men are much more optimistic than women about the possibility of acquiring a larger home (e.g., in 1998, 17 percent of men and 11 percent of women think this possibility is "very likely"). However, in the years between 1998 and 2001, both men and women become more optimistic about this possibility.

A fourth question asked in more than one survey year inquires whether the respondent thinks it is possible to achieve the American Dream. Men and women are equally likely to agree that it is possible in the 2001 survey (no significant difference is measured by the chi-square). Both are more likely to agree than to disagree. In 2001, only a small minority of respondents say that the American Dream does not exist (approximately 17 percent overall). However, in 2004, men and women diverge in their opinions on the possibility of achieving the American Dream. Men are significantly more likely to say that it is possible (80 percent vs. 65 percent). Survey results from 2009 reveal that, although a majority of men and women continue to believe they can achieve the American Dream, this majority is becoming increasingly small. The gender gap remains large in the 2009 surveys, with women being less optimistic. Little changes in survey responses on this question in the period between January and May 2009, but men and women did become a bit more optimistic.

Finally, the last item presented in Table 5.3 inquires about the ability of middle-class Americans to achieve the American Dream. Respondents are more optimistic in 2001 than they are in 2009, and men and women are similarly optimistic in the earlier (but not later) survey year. The changes in opinion on this item are among the largest observed in these analyses. In 2001, 72 percent of women agree that most middle-class Americans could achieve the American Dream. By January 2009, a minority of women (49 percent) agree with this statement, and that percentage remains stable in May 2009. Although men are more optimistic than women on this item in the two 2009 surveys, they also experience a considerable drop in optimism from the 2001 survey year.

Conclusions

A summary of U.S. men's and women's relative achievements in areas involving education, occupation, earnings, politics, and opportunity shows a gender divide that (in spite of progress) remains considerable. However, results from survey items on the American Dream collected by Zogby International show that a majority of both men and women continue to believe in the American Dream. Interestingly, men and women are more likely to see it as a spiritual dream rather than a material dream in most survey years. Gender contrasts do show that men believe in the Dream more than women do, and men are more likely to define it in material ways. Men and women show declining optimism in the surveys collected after the 2008 economic crisis. Women, however, are more optimistic about President Obama and his economic policies.

Although differences in men's and women's responses to the Zogby poll questions are often statistically significant, it is important to note that in most cases men and women show the same overall pattern of response. In early survey years (e.g., 2001), more gender differences exist in opinion on the definition of the American Dream than in opinion on the chance of one's family achieving this American Dream. In more recent survey years (e.g., 2009), men and women remain somewhat similar in their definitions of the Dream, but their goals in life have increasingly diverged, with men considerably more likely to say that their goals in life involve material success. The Zogby survey results support the larger research on gender differences in attitudes about inequality (e.g., Beutel and Marini 1995; Kane 2000) by showing that women are more likely than are men to see inequity in the Dream. They are also more likely than men to wonder about their chances (and the chances of most middle-class Americans) of achieving the Dream. The gender gap on these issues of achievement and equity is increasing. One of the largest changes in public opinion that is observed in the Zogby polls involves women's attitudes about middle-class Americans achieving the Dream. Almost three-fourths of women (72 percent) agree that most middle-class Americans can achieve the American Dream in the 2001 survey. This percentage drops to under 50 percent (49 percent) in January 2009 and remains at that percentage in the May 2009 survey.

The similar gender patterns and overall belief in the American Dream revealed in responses to many of the Zogby survey questions (especially in the earlier survey years) is interesting given evidence of a continued gender gap on indicators of achieving the Dream. There are a number of insights into this puzzle. One of the factors that might explain the juxtaposition of economic inequality for women and continued support of the Dream may have to do with how the Dream is defined. The Zogby data clearly show that, in spite of shifts toward a material definition, Americans (male and female, but especially female) tend to define the American Dream in spiritual (more than economic) terms.

Other insights into the findings on gender and the American Dream that are revealed in this chapter come from elsewhere. As Heather Johnson (author of *The American Dream and the Power of Wealth* [2006]) suggests, inequality in the land of the Dream is a hard pill to swallow. The American Dream is so much a part of the fabric of American society that we fail to question it (regardless of whether we have full access to it). We grew up on it. De Tocqueville noted the exceptional quality of Americans in their anticipation of success. Cullen (2003) and others have commented on the strength of this Dream through times of slavery and inequality. Lipset 1996 also notes the exceptionalism of American values and the notion that anyone can get ahead by working hard. Attitude surveys from other countries show much more support for the notion that working hard is sometimes not enough (Hanson, Kennelly, and Fuchs 2007; Kluegel and Smith 1986; Mason and Kluegel 2000). The resistance to questioning the American Dream, regardless of inequalities, is revealed in the Zogby data. This resistance may, however, be waning. Results from the Zogby American Dream surveys provide some support for those who have noted that the American Dream might unravel as we experience economic crisis, a growing wealth gap, expanding poor immigrant populations, and continued racism and sexism in American life. The Zogby polls show that men and women (but especially women) are increasingly less confident in this Dream.

Our research supports that of others (e.g., Jennifer Hochschild [1999] in *Facing up to the American Dream*) in providing evidence showing that women (as well as other minority groups) often believe in the Dream at least as much (if not more) than those who have more opportunity to achieve the Dream. Hochschild argues that this belief might provide motivation for achievement. To the extent that a belief in the Dream creates agency and effort toward upward mobility, it provides a positive function for all.

However, this shared belief in the Dream has another aspect. The cycle of inequality will continue when those who have achieved the Dream and those who have not agree on the greater worth of those who have achieved the American Dream. When this happens, people do not blame the structures that contribute to the inequality in the Dream, and change will be slow. Jimmy Carter (in his book *Our Endangered Values* [2005]) refers to this stagnation as a "moral crisis."

What can we do to close the gender gap in areas of life associated with the American Dream? Researchers and policy makers (e.g., Phyllis Moen and Patricia Roehling [2006]; Robert Drago [2007]) have provided a number of solutions, including:

- Allow flexible careers and occupational paths that acknowledge rather than ignore personal and family goals and obligations.
- Promote families and communities in our economic and legislative policies and practices, not just wealth accumulation. America needs a family policy.
- Enforce laws (e.g., Equal Pay Act, Title VII, Title IX) that prohibit gender inequality and sexual harassment in schools and in the workforce.
- Make sure that safety nets and federal assistance are available for single mothers and children of single mothers.
- Provide training and skills to poor women, especially those heading families. We need to do better at providing skills and jobs, not welfare and chronic poverty.

In the United States, considerable evidence shows that systems and structures work to the distinct advantage of some and the disadvantage of others. The American Dream suggests that all can succeed. Yet empirical evidence clearly shows that women have had less success than men in achieving the Dream. Our findings reveal that, although women and men believe in the American Dream, women are slightly less likely to define it in material ways and less likely to think that the Dream is possible. Johnson 2006 suggests that continued support of an equitable "American Dream" in the context of structured inequality is immoral and irresponsible. Others (e.g., Cullen 2003) have suggested that the growing disenchantment felt by increasing numbers of people who are denied access to the American Dream may, in the end, be a threat to our culture and way of life. Johnson 2006 critiques the inequities in the American Dream and asks, "Do we believe in the American Dream enough to make it real?"

Appendix: Methodology

Telephone Survey

Sampling. The majority of telephone lists for polls and surveys are produced in the IT department at Zogby International. Vendor-supplied lists are used for regions with complicated specifications, such as some congressional districts. Customer-supplied lists are used for special projects, such as customer-satisfaction surveys and organization-membership surveys.

Telephone lists generated in the IT department are called from versions of nationally published sets of phone CDs of listed households, ordered by telephone number. Residential (or business) addresses are selected and then coded by region, where applicable. An appropriate replicate (see the "Definitions" section) is generated from the (original) parent list of U.S. addresses and sampled multiple times.

Acquired lists are tested for duplicates, coded for region, tested for regional coverage, and ordered by telephone, as needed. The resulting list is loaded into the computer-assisted telephone interviewing (CATI; see the "Definitions" section) application, and the randomize function within the CATI software is run to further assure a good mix for the telephone list.

Interviewing. Interviews are conducted at Zogby International by professional interviewers trained on the CATI computer system. A policy requiring one supervisor to no more than twelve interviewers is used. The sample management module of the CATI system gives all prospective respondent households in the source telephone list the same chance of joining the sample. Regional quotas are employed to ensure adequate coverage nationwide.

Weighting. Reported frequencies and crosstabs are weighted using the appropriate demographic profile to provide a sample that best represents the targeted population from which the sample is drawn. The proportions composing the demographic profile are compiled from historical exit poll data, census data, and Zogby International survey data.

Sampling Error. "Sampling error," often referred to as the margin of error, is the percentage that survey results are likely to differ from the actual due to the size of the sample drawn. If a survey were conducted of all the members of a population, the sampling error would be zero. Other sources of possible error exist in survey research, such as sample design error and measurement error.

Definitions.

> *CATI (Computer-Aided Telephone Interview):* This software application displays survey questions to interviewers at LAN workstations, stores survey responses keyed in by the interviewer on a server, and manages list disposition.

> *Replicate:* This sublist shares the same cover characteristics as its parent list. Replicates are generated from the parent list by selecting every nth record from the parent list, where n is the size of the replicate divided by the total number of records in the parent list. Thus, a replicate is a portion of the parent list that is representative of the whole parent list.

Web Survey

Zogby International has assembled a database of individuals who have registered to take part in online polls through solicitations on the company's Web site as well as other Web sites that span the political spectrum—liberal, conservative, and middle of the road; politically active and apolitical; and easy to reach and hard to find. Many individuals who have participated in Zogby's telephone surveys also have submitted e-mail addresses so they may take part in online polls.

Political polling is not the only reason people have signed on to take part in the interactive surveys. Many have joined to participate in consumer research as well as surveys conducted in conjunction with such organizations as MSNBC. Zogby has taken strenuous efforts to ensure its interactive panel is as representative as possible. Individuals who registered were asked to provide personal information, such as home state, age, and political party, to Zogby, which in turn examined that data and contacted individuals by telephone to confirm that it was valid.

Respondents do not choose to take part in a poll: They are chosen at random by Zogby from a database of hundreds of thousands, much like the database of millions across the country who have telephones. Zogby Interactive respondents self-select which poll to participate in about as much as a person with a telephone could choose to call up Zogby and ask to be part of a poll. Further, Zogby telephones about 2 percent of respondents who completed the interactive survey to validate their personal data.

To solicit participation, Zogby sent e-mails to individuals who had asked to join its online-polling database, inviting them to complete an interactive poll. Interactive polls are supplemented by phone polls when needed to ensure proper demographic representation, especially among hard-to-reach groups. The interactive database is sampled whenever possible to keep responses fresh.

References

American Association for Public Opinion Research (AAPOR). 2000. *Standard definitions: Final dispositions of case codes and outcome rates of surveys.* Lenexa, KS: AAPOR.

American Association of University Women (AAUW). 2008. *Where the girls are: The facts about gender equity in education.* Washington, DC: AAUW.

Beutel, A. M., and M. M. Marini. 1995. Gender and values. *American Sociological Review* 60:436–448.

Carter, J. 2005. *Our endangered values: America's moral crisis.* New York: Simon and Schuster.

Center for Women and Politics. 2007. *Facts and Findings.* Available at www.cawp .rutgers.edu/tacts.html (accessed October 8, 2007).

Childstats.gov. 2008. *Child poverty.* Available at www.childstats.gov/americas Children/tables/econ1a.asap (accessed January 17, 2010).

Cullen, J. 2003. *The American Dream: A short history of and idea that shaped a nation.* New York: Oxford University Press.

Drago, R. 2007. *Striking a balance: Work, family, life.* Boston: Dollars and Sense.

Feminist Research Center. 2000. *Empowering women in business.* Arlington, VA: Feminist Majority Foundation.

Frey, W. H., B. A. Gresch, and J. Yeasting. 2001. *America by the Numbers: A field guide to the U.S. population.* New York: Free Press.

Garfinkle, N. 2006. *The American dream vs. the gospel of wealth.* New Haven, CT: Yale University Press.

Gilligan, C. 1982. *In a different voice.* Cambridge, MA: Harvard University Press.

Hanson, S. L. 2009. *Swimming against the tide: African American girls and science education.* Philadelphia, PA: Temple University Press.

Hanson, S. L., I. Kennelly, and S. Fuchs. 2007. Perceptions about fairness: Gender, and attitudes about opportunity among scientists in Germany and the U.S. *Journal of Women and Minorities in Science and Engineering* 13: 231–258.

Ho, A. K. 2007. *Achieving the American dream.* Lanham, MD: Hamilton Books.

Hochschild, J. L. 1995. *Facing up to the American dream.* Princeton, NJ: Princeton University Press.

Institute for Women's Public Policy Research. 2007. The gender wage ratio: Women's and men's earnings. Available at www.iwpr.org/pdf/C350.pdf (accessed January 15, 2010).

Inter-Parliamentary Union. 2009. *Women in Parliaments: World Classification.* Available at www.ipu.org/wmn-e/classif.htm (accessed January 15, 2010).

Johnson, H. B. 2006. *The American dream and the power of wealth: Choosing schools and inheriting wealth in the land of opportunity.* New York: Routledge.

Joint Center Data Bank. 2007. *Living arrangements of children.* Available at www.jointcenter.org/DB/factsheet/livarg.htm (accessed January 15, 2010).

Kane, E. W. 2000. Racial and ethnic variations in gender-related attitudes. *Annual Review of Sociology* 26:419–439.

Kluegel, J., and E. Smith. 1986. *Beliefs about inequality: Americans' views of what is and what ought to be.* Hawthorne, NY: Aldine De Gruyter.

Lewis, J. J. 2007. *Women prime ministers and presidents—20th century heads of state.* Available at http://womenshistory.about.com/od/rulers20th/women_heads.htm?p=1 (accessed September 25, 2007).

Lindsey, L. 2005. *Gender roles: A sociological perspective.* Upper Saddle River, NJ: Prentice Hall.

Lipset, S. M. 1996. *American exceptionalism: A double edged sword.* New York: Norton.

Mason, D. S., and J. R. Kluegel. 2000. *Marketing democracy: Changing opinion about inequality and politics in east central Europe.* New York: Rowan and Littlefield.

McKinnon, J. 2003. *The black population in the United States: March 2002.* U.S. Census Bureau, Current Population Reports, Series P20-541, Washington, DC.

Moen, P., and P. Roehling. 2005. *The career mystique: Cracks in the American dream.* Lanham, MD: Rowman and Littlefield.

Murphy, E., and E. J. Graff. 2009. Are you paid as much as a man if he had your job? Available at www.womensmedia.com/money/95-gender-wage-gap-are-you-paid-as-much-as-a-man-if-he-had-your-job.html (accessed December 7, 2010).

National Center for Poverty. 2009. *Poverty in the United States: Frequently asked questions.* Available at www.wpc.umich.edu/poverty (accessed January 8, 2010).

National Coalition for Women and Girls in Education. 2008. *Title IX at 35: Beyond the headlines.* Available at www.ncwge.org/PDF/TitleIXat35.pdf (accessed January 1, 2010).

National Committee on Pay Equity. 2009. *Questions and answers on pay equity.* Available at www.pay-equity.org/info-Q&A.html (accessed January 1, 2010).

National Science Foundation (NSF). 2008. *Women, minorities, and persons with disabilities in science and engineering.* Arlington, VA: NSF.

Newman, K. S. 1993. *Declining fortunes: The withering of the American dream.* New York: Basic Books.

Osborne, J. W. 2001. Testing stereotype threat: Does anxiety explain race and sex differences in achievement? *Contemporary Educational Psychology* 26, no. 3: 291–310.

Prettyman, S. S. 1998. Discourses on adolescence, gender, and schooling: An overview. *Educational Studies: A Journal in the Foundations of Education* 29, no. 4: 329–340.

Riordan, C. 2002. What do we know about the effects of single-sex schools in the private sector? Implications for public schools. In *Gender in Policy and Practice: Perspectives on Single-Sex and Coeducational Schooling,* ed. A. Datnow and L. Hubbard, 10–30. New York: Routledge/Falmer.

Shapiro, T. M. 2004. *The hidden cost of being African American: How wealth perpetuates inequality.* New York: Oxford University Press.

Sheppard, J. M., and S. Haas. 2003. *Cooperation tracking study: April 2003 update.* Cincinnati, OH: Council for Marketing and Opinion Research.

Sherraden, M. W. 1991. *Assets and the poor.* Armonk, NY: M. E. Sharpe.

Wallechinsky, D. 2007. *Is America still no. 1?* Available at www.parade.com/articles/editions/2007/edition_01-14-2007 (accessed October 8, 2007).

Women's Sports Foundation. 1997. *Gender equity report card: A survey of athletic opportunity in American higher education.* East Meadow, NY: Women's Sports Foundation.

———. 2002. *Title IX at 30: Athletics receive C+.* East Meadow, NY: Women's Sports Foundation.

CHAPTER 6

 # Want Meets Necessity in the New American Dream

John Zogby

U TICA, NEW YORK, is not known as a trend-setting community. However, having lived there all my life and establishing a polling and research company, I found it a perfect place to see the evolving American Dream.

Utica, located in Oneida County in the dead center of New York State, grew because of the Erie Canal and prospered as a mill town and later with factories owned by GE, Bendix, and other manufacturers. (Zogby International operates out of a former GE aerospace plant.) The job exodus began in the 1960s, and the population has dropped from one hundred thousand to the current sixty thousand. Here, we knew hard times before they became in vogue.

Back in 1987, my wife, Kathy, and I began a study of hunger in Oneida County, using telephone and door-to-door interviews. We asked if anyone in the household had "not eaten any food in any twenty-four-hour period during the past year because of a lack of money." The resulting 21 percent who said "yes" surprised us; but what really took us aback in a separate telephone sample of 800 was finding that 3.6 percent of people in households earning from $50,000 to $75,000 were in that group, as were 3.2 percent of those earning more than $75,000. Remember that this was during the 1980s, when those were solid middle-class incomes.

These were mostly people who had lost higher-paying jobs and had to adjust to their new reality. They did not want to give up their homes and still had to own cars. Their children still had the same needs. Food was the one trade-off.

In 1990, one in seven people nationwide reported earning less than they once did. Now, it is more than one in four. Many Americans are now in their second or third generation of downward spiraling jobs. Places like Utica were indeed the trendsetters for the growing number of no-longer-booming communities.

If the American Dream was all about money and material goods, then it should have been in trouble in Utica twenty years ago and wilting everywhere in the recession-cum-depression of 2008–2009. What I saw anecdotally in my hometown twenty years ago gave me a heads-up that the American Dream was not dying; it was just changing. Now, that is happening everywhere among Americans across all demographic groups.

Uticans accepted years ago that the economy would never return to where it once was, and people internalized that. I saw Elisabeth Kübler-Ross's stages of grief impacting an entire community: from shock, anger, despair, and resignation to an acceptance of diminished economic circumstances and an adjustment of what the good life might mean.

However, one's own economic outlook is just one piece of how people have redefined the American Dream. The shift has happened in far more prosperous places than Utica, well before the housing bubble burst and banks collapsed. Although most Americans remain active consumers, many have found the acquisitive life failing to meet fundamental human needs. That is the other and perhaps most important element of the new American Dream.

It is frankly not what I expected when I set out to measure attitudes toward a concept so central to how people see themselves and their society. Years ago, when I first thought about a book on the topic, I anticipated data that would force me to paint a pessimistic picture of Americans. Instead, I found quite the opposite. Readers and reviewers of that book, *The Way We'll Be: The Zogby Report on the Transformation of the American Dream,* often come away believing I see the world through rose-colored glasses. That is not me. Remember, I grew up in a place that, in addition to having lost its economic mojo forty years ago, averages 207 cloudy days per year.

My observations on the new American Dream are not about me. They are about the opinions voiced by thousands of people over a number of years of scientific polling.

The New American Dream: Secular Spiritualism

In 1998, I started to survey perceptions of the American Dream nationally. Did people believe it was possible for them and others to achieve? What did it mean to them? Was it material success or fulfillment in other ways? Do some people believe the material American Dreams are not in the cards for them but might be for their children? Finally, how many had given up on the very idea of a particular American Dream?

Our key question offered four statement agreement choices, each yielding a type of American Dreamer or nonbeliever:

Traditional Materialist: I believe the American Dream means material success. It is possible for me and my family and for most middle-class Americans to achieve.

Secular Spiritualists: I believe you can achieve the American Dream through spiritual fulfillment rather than material success.

Deferred Dreamers: I believe the American Dream means material success. It exists but is more likely to be attained by my children and not me.

Dreamless Dead: I believe I cannot achieve the American Dream, whether material or spiritual, nor can most middle-class Americans.

Over time, we have seen a steady movement from the Traditional Materialist to the Secular Spiritualist. In a June 2007 interactive poll, the two categories were tied. However, in a 2008 postelection interactive poll of nearly twenty-five thousand voters, the two switched places.

Nov. 2008: Attitudes defining the American Dream

Secular Spiritualists	37%
Traditional Materialists	27%
Deferred Dreamers	8%
Dreamless Dead	12%

It comes as no surprise that people who frequently attend religious services make up 44 percent of Secular Spiritualists. However, 33 percent of Secular Spiritualists rarely or never attend services. More than religion, these Secular Spiritualists demonstrate an acceptance of a world with limits and a longing for a simpler life. Looking more broadly, we see Secular Spiritualists coming from several directions.

The Sources of a Redefined Dream

We can look at these Secular Spiritualists through specific, poll-driven demographics but more interestingly through social trends and generational changes.

The first is one we have already talked about: those whose reduced expectations have been forced upon them by the loss of higher-paying jobs. These were the angry male voters of the 1990s. Over time, their acceptance becomes more complete, anger diminishes, and the realization cannot be denied that food must still be put on the table and that life goes on. Their world has changed, and there is no use fighting it.

These folks are the core group of new consumers. They say: I have a shrinking dollar, so you are going to have to give me the best I can get for it. They have helped pave the way for the retail dominance of Walmart, Costco, and Target. Retailers have been forced to adapt. Here is an example that hit home for me. Twenty or so years ago when I bought my young sons a bucket of Kentucky Fried Chicken, it cost $21.99. Now, you get it for $7.99.

Next come those who have discovered that having more does not lead to a fuller life. In a June 2007 Zogby Interactive survey, we explored people's expectations for their careers and possessions. Specifically, we asked people if their expectations for their careers and possessions had increased, decreased, or stayed the same over the past few years. Here is the result: 31 percent increased, 22 percent decreased, and 41 percent stayed the same. We then asked those with decreased expectations to choose three possible reasons why. Here are the choices and results:

June 2007: Why do you have decreased expectations?

Realized I couldn't attain my goals	26%
Working at a job that paid less than previous job	28%
Want a simpler life	36%

Those who want a simpler life represent millions of people who want out of the rat race. They are saying that they have enough or too much. They do not need the latest iteration of the iPhone or another addition to the house. Instead, they are choosing family, hobbies, and volunteer work.

Here are the groups most likely to want a simpler life (for each, more than 40 percent expressed that choice): rural dwellers, people living in households that include a union member, people ages eighteen to twenty-seven, libertarians, people with incomes of $50,000 to $75,000, Hispanics, Asians, and people joined in civil unions. You would be very hard-pressed to develop a stereotype from those cohorts. Instead, they represent their own demographic of people who look inside for motivation and identity instead of how high they have climbed the ladder of material possessions.

The next source of Secular Spiritualists is generational. In keeping with our Baby Boomer image, I shall start with my own. I call us "Woodstockers." We are the generation that defined ourselves as "Youth" and had a hard time letting go. We set out to change the world. You can judge whether we did, and if it was for better or worse. Now, as our ages hit the late fifties and early sixties, we need a second act, and we have a lot of time on our hands to play it out.

We will be the first age cohort where millions will live to be one hundred. What to do with all that time? Robert Fogel estimates that "vol-work" (as opposed to "earn work") will add up to millions of hours that the Woodstockers can use to help their communities and to give meaning and success to their lives.

We already have a role model, the Private Generation whose attitudes were formed by post–World War II America and are now the bulk of retirees exploring how to give back and to enjoy the last third of life.

Now let us look at the future and the permanence of Secular Spiritualists. These are young people ages eighteen to thirty whom I call the "First Global Generation"™. The twenty-something stereotype paints a youth culture obsessed with the latest hot new thing in style, technology, or other consumer-driven ID tag. Instead, this age cohort has accepted Secular Spiritualism in the same numbers as their elders. What makes them tick? They are connected to the rest of the world like no other generation. They are multicultural and accepting. Because of travel and social networking, their friends can be anywhere in the world. Here are a few examples of what our surveys have found about First Globals:

- Fifty-six percent have passports.
- One in four expects to live and to work in a foreign country.
- Ninety percent see Mexicans as hard-working.
- They want free trade, but only if agreements protect workers.

- They are as much libertarian as liberal, but most value problem solving over orthodoxy.
- They are basically prochoice but judge the morality of abortion based on the specific circumstance.
- They favor a multilateral foreign policy.
- They are the "green" generation, favoring the Kyoto Treaty and other steps to slow global warming.

For these young Americans, Secular Spiritualism is not an adaptation to a sour economy but is instead formative. Nearly four in ten First Globals identify as Secular Spiritualists. They are unlikely to change as they get older. In fact, the opposite should occur, as maturity and realities should move many of their peers away from being materialists and toward the views of Secular Spiritualists. Also, the same technological and social changes that produced the First Globals should similarly impact today's adolescents.

Before we leave generations, what about the cohort who came after the Woodstockers and before the First Globals? I call its members the "Nike Generation" for their "just do it" attitude. Despite having been born into a world of presidential scandals, assassinations, oil embargoes, record-high divorce rates, and AIDS, their attitudes about the American Dream are very similar to those of the Woodstockers and First Globals.

The final force shaping Secular Spiritualism is not new. It is the American spirit of sacrifice for the greater good that has always tempered raw materialism.

In my early years of polling, I did work for municipalities who wanted to know how willing people would be to recycle. Government officials were very skeptical that citizens would be willing to sort and to recycle their trash, but our surveys found just the opposite. Give the American people a just cause, a clear rationale, and strong leadership, and they will do the right thing. In the 1970s, two presidents asked us to lower the thermostat and to conserve energy, and we did it.

It is easier to accept less and to look for gratification in the nonmaterial when you see others doing the same, and they are doing it because it is simply the right thing to do.

Nonbelievers in the Dream and President Obama

Not everyone is as optimistic about the American Dream as our Secular Spiritualists, especially the 12 percent who do not believe that they or most middle-class Americans can achieve it. Who are they? First off, they were instrumental in electing Barack Obama. He won the votes of 71 percent of those who say the American Dream does not exist and 68 percent of those who are not sure. John McCain would be in the White House if only people who believed in the American Dream voted.

The numbers are not about Obama's voting pull with minorities. We found no racial difference on whether the American Dream is attainable. The "Dreamless Dead" are more likely to be low income, but there is no straight line correlation as incomes rise. Given the election results, it is no surprise that nonbelievers in the Dream are more likely to be politically liberal.

Lest you think that Obama, a man who promoted hope and change, is simply the electoral product of pessimism, you should note that he did win 45 percent of Secular Spiritualists. It is clear that he wants to win over (or at least to soften the opposition of) evangelical Christians. Obama's comfort in using the religious vernacular of the black church and his call for mutual sacrifice has some appeal to evangelicals.

Digging Deeper

In a January 2009 Zogby Interactive poll of nearly 3,500 likely voters, Zogby International offered respondents reasons why they might believe or disbelieve in their chances of achieving the American Dream and asked them to choose the two that most applied.

Our poll revealed that the objective reality of current job or financial situations was not at all the prime reason for the chosen response. Instead, respondents' main reasons for belief in the Dream were faith in themselves and the American ideal of opportunity for those who work for it. Those who said the American Dream did not exist were most likely to blame the powerful who did not care about them. Next was rejection of the idea of U.S. exceptionalism. Only 8 percent rejected the American Dream because they have been forced to take lower-paying jobs.

Here are the top reasons for believing in the American Dream:

59 percent: "I'm intelligent and work hard, so I should succeed."
52 percent: "America is the land of opportunity."
25 percent: "I am an optimist."
25 percent: "I have a secure job or business."
15 percent: "My religious faith ensures I will find fulfillment."
 2 percent: Not sure or other.

Here are the reasons given by those who say the Dream does not exist:

44 percent: "The powers that be don't care about people like me."

29 percent: "Americans shouldn't think of themselves as special and entitled to an ideal life."

27 percent: "Where I live, it costs too much, and the American Dream is just out of reach."

14 percent: Not sure or other.

10 percent: "I am a pessimist."

8 percent: "I have been forced to take a lower-paying job."

7 percent: "I don't have enough education and can't afford to go back to school."

7 percent: "I recently lost my job and am out of work."

This survey showed some predictable political, religious, and generational differences. For example, among believers:

- Sixty-one percent of Republicans cited "America is the land of opportunity."
- Forty-nine percent of frequent churchgoers attributed their optimism to their religious faith.
- Seventy-six percent of people under age thirty said their brains and hard work will bring them success.

For those who reject the American Dream:

- Forty-six percent of those younger than age thirty believed that Americans are not entitled to a better life, which fits perfectly into their overall more-global outlook.
- Forty-four percent of the same age group said that the cost of living is just too high for them to achieve the dream.
- Conservatives were about ten points more likely than liberals to say that the powerful do not care about them.
- Liberals were thirteen points more likely than conservatives to say that Americans should not think of themselves as special and entitled to an ideal life.

Attitudes about the American Dream are based on how people perceive themselves, America, and the major institutions that shape our lives. For many years now, people have increasingly expressed frustration with government, business, education, media, not-for-profits, and organized religions. This is a huge concern, because so many who reject the ideal of the American Dream also feel powerless. Most people want the opportunity to succeed, however they define it. They just ask that our major institutions give them a fair shake.

Regardless of whether you consider the American Dream to be something special to this nation or you see it as a fanciful, unrealistic, or chauvinistic notion, it behooves us all to maintain a society where everyone perceives the opportunity to succeed.

The American Dream and Mr. Obama

Our presidents are articulators of the American Dream. They must judge how voters define it and have a vision for how it can be reached. If these were ordinary times, Obama's personal story and verbal ability to inform might be enough for him to lead the growing number of Secular Spiritualists. Instead, Obama is navigating in waters different than any other U.S. leader.

The closest comparison is to Franklin D. Roosevelt and his stewardship during the Great Depression. It is not a perfect analogy. This is a very different nation than the one Roosevelt took over in 1936. Roosevelt's New Deal programs and those that followed thirty years later under Lyndon B. Johnson's Great Society built a social safety net that did not exist in the 1930s. To be sure, holes exist in the net that too many still fall through, but far fewer Americans fear hunger and homelessness now than they did then.

In fact, being poor today is nothing like the poverty of the Depression. The 2005 U.S. Census found that among people living below the poverty line, these percentages owned the following: refrigerators, 99 percent; stoves and color TVs, 98 percent; microwaves, 93 percent; VCRs, 88 percent; vehicles, 86 percent; stereo systems, 73 percent; and computers, 59 percent.

Hardly anyone anticipates losing those things. They are anxious about jobs, health care, and housing.

FDR followed a strategy of relief, followed by recovery and reform. Obama is following that model but also sees speeding reform out of necessity. Obama sought relief immediately, with job creation the number-one priority and rationale for a $787-billion stimulus bill. The vast sums going to banks were aimed at stabilizing the housing market. In March 2010, Obama signed two pieces of legislation into law to reform health care. Voters were never clear about the specific direction they favored for major reforms, but they clearly wanted change. The president suffered from too many crises all at once that needed his attention, a majority of voters who felt that they had not seen enough improvement in their lives despite trillions of public dollars being spent, and hyperpartisanship in Congress that made any attempt to produce change a bitter and divided process. For these reasons and some real mistakes made by the president himself, voters rejected Obama's political party in the November 2010 elections. History may just prove kinder to him.

In a February 2009 interactive survey, 16 percent of people said that during the past year, they or a member of their household had gone without medical or prescription drug care due to cost. That number was 34 percent for households earning less than $25,000 per year but was 10 percent for those above $100,000. For good reason, many people, even those in the middle class, worry about losing health care benefits and having to forego treatment even if they have some level of insurance. Although Obama talks about fixing an expensive health care system as an economic and human necessity, it also would calm one of people's greatest anxieties and threats to the American Dream.

In that same survey, 11 percent had failed to make a mortgage or rent payment on time due to lack of funds. Little significant difference emerged across income groups. The number was 15 percent for those earning less than $25,000 and 9 percent for those above $100,000. Losing your home is obviously traumatic. People fear being forced to live in another neighborhood. Some of this is status and self-image, but it is also about their children and wanting them to have the best social and educational surroundings.

In March 2010, I completed a new round of polling on the American Dream. Past Zogby polls have shown considerable hope in the American Dream. For example, in 2001 76 percent of Americans believed it was possible for themselves and their families to achieve the American Dream. This number remained somewhat high (67 percent) following the 2008 elections. The March 2010 poll showed a significant dip, however, with a small majority of Americans (57 percent) still believing that the American Dream was possible for their family.

· Although the numbers on Secular Spiritualists, Traditional Materialists, and Deferred Dreamers remained more or less stable compared to

November 2010, the percentage of Dreamless Dead jumped from 12 to 20 percent. We found this pessimism increasing across all demographic groups. Predictably, the jump was greatest among those earning the least (annual household income below $25,000), going from 19 to 44 percent. Other groups that also had higher increases of Dreamless Dead included women, political independents, and those without college degrees.

Clearly, a very weak job market is the prime cause for this loss of hope. Several polls released during the fall of 2010 by Zogby International and other pollsters found that more than one in four middle-income Americans and two in five lower-income earners said someone in their household has been laid off or has lost a job in the last year. In a recent ABC/*Washington Post* survey, 57 percent of middle-income Americans and 68 percent of lower earners said the U.S. economy is in "long-term decline." Equally ominous, the percentage of those American adults working at a job that pays less than a previous job rose to 35 percent in a March 2009 poll.

It certainly seems as though people see the current recession as more than just a down period in the normal business cycle. I have written columns about the deep loss of confidence in our major institutions, especially in big business, banks, and government. Actions taken by leaders in the business and the political realms have given people in the political center, left, and the right very good reason to lose faith. They can cite their own litanies of what they see as failure and even contempt from the nation's most powerful people.

More alarming may be the self-fulfilling prophecies that this skepticism cultivates. For the economy, people are more likely to hunker down and to diminish any chance that consumer spending will restart the economy. For government, cynicism moves people away from the process, pushing political discourse further to the extremes and making government even more dysfunctional and less responsive that it already is. None of this can be separated from rapid and all-encompassing technological change that is altering our personal and institutional relationships. Inevitably, our institutions must change to keep up.

I am an optimist. The American Dream is a deeply American concept, and although its meaning may be adapted to new circumstances, the American Dream will endure. I am particularly optimistic for the young generation. When I think about America and its Dream and about those who will sort through and find solutions, I think of the under-thirty generation I call First Globals. What Winston Churchill said in

1947 is still true: "Democracy is the worst form of government, except for all those other forms that have been tried from time to time." It may take some time, but the generation that has grown up wired, connected, and open to the world will make our institutions responsive again and perhaps will create new ones. They will also keep the American Dream alive and continue the path that defines it not as material but as personal and spiritual fulfillment. Carpe diem.

So as much as people say they want simpler and fuller lives, anxieties about jobs, health care, and housing upend that American Dream. We can only hope that leaders in government and business and the people find solutions that reduce those concerns for as many as possible. Talk is cheap. The nation needs results, and the buck still stops at the president's desk.

Americans should also come to grips with a new reality where excess is no longer sustainable. In fact, sustainability is becoming the watchword of the twenty-first century. We have come to this point by choice (the simpler life people want) and by necessity (global warming and the emerging economic power and needs of the developing world).

This is where Obama has the skills to lead. People want a government that is fair and provides opportunity. They do not want a handout for themselves or anyone else (witness displeasure at the banking bailout). They will no longer tolerate our current level of economic inequality, even though they may not express it exactly that way.

It seems to me that these concepts were the foundation of Obama's campaign and of his first days in office. They are reinforced by his life story and up-by-the-bootstraps rise from community organizer to leader of the free world. His election as our first African American president inspires millions, especially our First Globals. In attitude and background, Obama shares much with this younger generation.

Presidents only attain greatness when the nation is under duress. Obama has that opportunity. Perhaps his most important measure will be whether he helped preserve the American Dream and steered it further in the direction of personal fulfillment.

CHAPTER 7

 **Religion and
the American Dream**

A Catholic Reflection
in a Generational Context

William V. D'Antonio

I N THIS CHAPTER, I explore the meaning and experience of the American Dream as it was perceived and lived out during the twentieth century for those Tom Brokaw has called the "Greatest Generation" and as it is currently perceived and experienced by those I call the "Millennial Generation." The former are people who came of age during the Great Depression and World War II. The latter are those who have come of age with the experience of September 11, the Iraq and Afghanistan wars, and now the greatest economic downturn since the Great Depression through which their grandparents lived. Within that context, I will reflect on how the Roman Catholic Church in the United States might have impacted the lives of American Catholics in their quest for the American Dream. This comparison of the grandparents with the grandchildren affords an opportunity to examine the American Dream as it has been lived throughout a period now of a full century.

According to Katharine O. Seelye (2009), "the phrase, 'the American dream' is generally agreed to have been coined first in 1931, in the midst of the Depression. In his book, *The Epic of America,* the historian James Truslow Adams wrote, 'It is not a dream of motor cars and high wages merely, but a dream of social order in which each man and each woman shall be able to attain the fullest stature of which they are innately capable.'"

In this chapter, I address this question: Is the social order that Adams saw as the grounding that would enable each person to achieve his or her maximum potential perceived to be relevant in this quest to Americans in general and Catholics in particular of the two generations noted? Do pollsters even ask that question? Or do the questions asked in most polls focus on the Dream as an individual goal or achievement? And, finally, what difference does it make? I take the phrase "social order" to refer to the institutional factors that may enhance or inhibit the quest for the Dream—in this chapter, church, government, and economy.

Most of the Brokaw generation began their lives as immediate descendents of the primarily white-ethnic European migration (1870–1925) and experienced the Depression of the 1930s, then World War II and its aftermath—the GI Bill, the baby boom, and the suburbanization of American life. Their grandchildren, the Millennials, were born into a post–Vietnam War world that has morphed into a seemingly endless series of wars that are fought at a distance involving a volunteer military. But they are also a generation in which more than a third achieved a college-plus education and experienced almost universal access to the Internet, the iPod, and all the technologies that link them to a rapidly globalizing world. They also were witness to the events of September 11 and their consequences and, especially for young Catholics, the sexual-abuse scandal that became widely known early in 2002. Moreover, they are the first generation to give majority support to same-sex marriage. Now, of course, they confront an economic meltdown that may be as traumatic for them as the Great Depression was for their grandparents. This combination of physical destruction, sexual abuse, wars without end, and an economic downturn that will not be easy to overcome poses financial, physical, and mental costs embedded in a social order that may threaten if not derail the quest for the Dream. This may be especially the case because of the way in which our social order is perceived across generations.

Background: A Version of the American Dream during the Great Depression

I begin my reflection on the Dream by returning to a date some seventy-plus years ago (1937), when my sixth-grade public school teacher asked me to recite a poem in honor of George Washington's birthday. The poem was written in the manner of how a first-generation Italian-American father might speak to his young son. So, with apologies to my ancestors, I offer you a few words from the past:

U know wat for isa schul keep out disa holiday, my son? No?
Wal, den, I gonna tell u bouta dessa Giorgio Washeenton.
Wal Giorgio wassa littla kid—hesa liv longa time ago—

The poem goes on to tell the story of the cherry tree and the lesson learned. It ends:

An' maybe so like Giorgio, you grow for be so great,
You gonna be da president, of dese Unita Stata.

—From my personal files

My sixth-grade class was a mix of Italian and Irish second- and third-generation Americans, with one Jewish boy and a few Protestants, all white. What did this poem mean to them or to me? I have no recollection of its possible message, only that I took pride in the way I said it, with the proper Italian American accent. And I never forgot it.

In retrospect, the message of the poem seems to be that if you go to school, work hard, and do not lie—that is, if you play by the rules—you can achieve whatever goal you may set for yourself. Many Americans perceived that a contemporary version of that poem was acted out during the Democratic primary campaign and election of 2008. Indeed, Senators Barack Obama and Hillary Clinton referred to it. Senator Obama made the point that "only in America could such a thing as a person named Barack Obama run for president." That his run resulted in his presidential election seemed to validate the Dream in the eyes of millions. The euphoria of the evening of November 4, 2008, in Grant Park, Chicago, Illinois, when Obama acknowledged his election was in the minds of millions a further validation of the Dream. But Obama's achievement was due to more than innate potential. He was not born poor: He had intelligent, well-educated parents; enjoyed a good prep-school education, with devoted grandparents taking care of him during crucial years; and benefited from excellent education at Columbia and Harvard to go with his high intellect. And he greatly benefited from the 1965 Voting Rights Law, a superb campaign organization, and a skilled team that knew how to organize through the Internet. Still, stories like Obama's make it difficult for Americans to appreciate the social institutions and organizations that make society and its dreams possible. I suggest some of the resulting negative consequences of seeing the Dream as essentially an individual achievement. Given the limitations of time and space, I can only hope to sketch out some of the dimensions of the problem with the American Dream as it has been developed and sustained over the years.

My Catholic and cross-generational overview includes the following:

1. A brief review of the history of the struggle of Roman Catholic leaders (church and lay) in the United States to adapt their teachings and practices to American society, especially to establish a Catholic school system to protect the lives and souls of Catholics from the perceived dangers of the then-dominant Protestant ethos
2. Use of polls of the general American population, including American Catholics, regarding their perception and achievement of the American Dream
3. A descriptive analysis of how American Catholics across the two generations have fared in their efforts to realize the Dream in their own lives
4. Observations on how Americans, including Catholics, perceive the contributions that such institutions as the government may or may not make to the achievement of the Dream, including the laws, teachings, and practices fostered by these institutions and their probable impact on achieving the Dream

The Catholic Church and the American Dream

In the first two centuries of the existence of the thirteen colonies, Roman Catholics, like Jews, Quakers, and other religious minorities, faced difficult challenges to their freedom to worship. The Protestants fleeing from England and other parts of Europe to seek religious freedom in the colonies were more concerned about protecting their own freedom than in helping others seek and find theirs (D'Antonio and Hoge 2006). The founding fathers of this country had come to appreciate the dangers of having established religions, or even one established religion, as they learned from the experience of European countries. This realization is seen in their writing of the Constitution and the Bill of Rights: The First Amendment to the Constitution disestablished any and all religions and further established that religion was not to be a test for citizenship or for holding public office. But that act of law did not end the encroachments on the freedom of Catholics and others to worship and to pass on their faith to the next generation.

The United States grew in population and land size in the nineteenth century, and so did the idea of tax-funded public schools: "However, these [schools] included a 'common core' of religious education based on Protestant teachings and ethics as well as a curriculum intended to inculcate students into the practice of 'American' traditions, which were often greatly influenced by Protestant, Anglo-Saxon traditions. This led to resentment and resistance on the part of Catholic laity and Church leadership alike" (Froehle and Gautier 2000, 64–65). In this new land of opportunity, Church leaders were determined that education should not include Protestantizing the growing waves of Catholic immigrants. As the waves of immigrants from all over Europe increased in numbers during the nineteenth century, so, too, did the growing number of Roman Catholic bishops concerned with their physical and spiritual well-being. A series of Plenary Councils focused attention on the threats these public schools posed and the Protestant ethos that permeated so much of American life, thus creating the need for the Church to have its own schools to mitigate these dangers. At the Third Plenary Council held in Baltimore in November and December 1884, the seventy-one bishops and archbishops of the council mandated the establishment of a school in every parish, the obligation of every pastor and of the parishioners to support the school, and the requirement that parents send their children to parochial schools. In the words of Bishop Bernard McQuaid of Rochester, "Raising and strengthening the walls of the Catholic fortress by building Catholic schools would serve to protect children from the 'wolves of the world' that were 'destroying countless numbers of the unguarded ones'" (Ibid., 65). Over time, ethnic (especially German, Irish, Polish, and French) and nonethnic schools were established to serve the interests of the Church and the growing numbers of immigrants. For the Church, the schools ensured the passing on of the faith, while for the major ethnic groups, they meant saving core aspects of their particular cultures and languages, at least for another generation or two.

Catholic elementary and high school enrollments reached their peak in the 1960s; almost half the Catholic student population and "12 percent of all elementary and secondary students in the United States, roughly 5.5 million students, were enrolled in over 13,000 Catholic schools in 1965" (Ibid., 68). In the forty years since then, a variety of factors, economic and social, has seen the decline in the number of parishes still operating schools. The proportion of Catholics enrolled in first grade dropped from its high in the 1960s to 23 percent in 1999, to

19 percent in 2004, and to 17 percent in 2006 (Gray and Gautier 2006). Stern 2007 reported that only 15 percent of Catholic students were enrolled in Catholic schools.

Many factors have influenced the decline in the number of parochial schools as we move into the twenty-first century. The Second Vatican Council documents encouraged engagement with the larger world; the guarantees of freedom of religion and conscience as well as the greater emphasis on personal responsibility for their actions may all have led many parents to decide that the public schools were no longer a threat to their faith. The nuns that once dominated the teaching staffs of these private schools at a very low financial cost are no longer readily available. And an important consequence of Catholics' moving to the suburbs has been the abandonment and closing of urban Catholic schools; the Millennial Generation has had less access to Catholic schools than its parents and grandparents had.

The picture at the college/university level has its own complications. Catholic college and university enrollments grew from 230,000 in 1950 to almost 700,000 in 1998 (Froehle and Gautier 2000, 79–80). By comparison, in 1950, higher-education enrollment for the United States stood at 2.7 million, while in 2000 it had reached and leveled off at 14.6 million. Thus, in 1950, Catholic college enrollment was 11 percent of the national total; in 2000, although it more than tripled in growth, it was only 5 percent of the total enrollment. As a consequence, many public state universities boast numbers of Catholics enrolled that well exceed even the number of Catholics at such schools as Notre Dame or Boston College. With ever-growing numbers in public and other private colleges and universities (Catholic and not), Millennial Catholics became the Catholic generation with the highest number of college-educated members in American history.

In December 1999, Bishop Joseph A. Fiorenza, as president of the United States Council of Catholic Bishops, looked back with great pride on that Third Plenary Council of 1884 and its decision to build a Catholic school system and to establish the Catholic University of America in Washington, D.C. The decision had proven itself by its ability to maintain Catholic identity through education. Indeed, as the Church prepared itself for the twenty-first century, Bishop Fiorenza declared that the Catholic school system had "been one of the glories of the Catholic experience in the United States" (Fiorenza 1999, 2). And so it was that for millions of American Catholics, and a growing number of non-

Catholics, the Catholic school system had proven itself a vehicle for educating a significant portion of the American population. In the process, they helped close the gap with other Americans of all religious groups in the percentage of Americans of all religious groups graduating from college (D'Antonio et al. 1996, 10–11). The general population of Catholics now has educational, occupational, and income levels on a par with other Americans. To the extent that American Catholics believe in the Dream, these findings suggest that the Dream may have meant much more than just owning a home. The building of the Catholic school system was a communal experience, with Episcopal leadership providing the institutional support, hundreds of thousands of religious women who devoted their lives with little or no financial recompense, and millions of Catholics whose financial giving was often made not from their surplus but from their substance. Indeed, there is a certain irony in the fact that Catholics in the suburbs today with higher incomes and more discretionary funds than their forbearers have been less willing to pay the price to build the schools for the twenty-first century. And so the question arises as to whether they may have become more self-centered than community-centered in their perspectives as they go about living the middle-class suburban way.

When the Catholic school system was first established, the leaders' dream was that all Catholics would attend their local Catholic schools. That was part of their dream was never fully realized. But evidence abounds that the system the bishops did create has been successful by most American standards.

Two surveys taken in 2005 illustrate the roles the Catholic schools played: One was the fourth national representative sample of American Catholics, and the second was a representative sample of Catholics who were members of Voice of the Faithful (VOTF), a national social movement formed in response to the 2002 sex-abuse scandal that promoted reform of the Catholic Church.[1] The difference in the number who attended Catholic schools among VOTF Catholics compared with the national sample of Catholics was striking:

---

[1] Two other surveys of American Catholics taken by the author (one in 1996–1997 of Call to Action Catholics and the second of Intentional Eucharistic Communities in the fall of 2008) produced results similar to the findings in the VOTF survey. These subsamples of Catholics had high levels of Catholic and advanced education, high income, high commitment to the Catholic Church, high Mass attendance rates, and high levels of discontent with what they described as an authoritarian hierarchy.

Comparing Levels of Catholic Education

	VOTF Catholics	Catholics, national sample
Catholic elementary school	70%	49%
Catholic high school	62%	29%
Catholic college/university	57%	12%

Among those factors that related to the spiritual aspects of life, the following religious behaviors and attitudes stand out:

Comparing Religious Behavior and Attitudes

	VOTF Catholics	Catholics, national sample
Marriage recognized by the Catholic Church	92%	73%
Weekly mass attendance	65%	34%
Prayer at least daily	79%	63%
Catholic Church among most important influences	62%	44%
Registered membership in a parish	85%	68%

Thus, insofar as these features of Catholic life reflect on the spiritual aspects, Catholic education seems to have made a difference in their church-related behavior (D'Antonio and Pogorelc 2007, 230, table A).

Catholics of my generation (grandparents) came of age as Catholic schools and Catechism classes for public-school Catholics were having a great impact. The Church's monarchical hierarchy set our spiritual goals in life; in terms of the aphorism of the time, it was "go to Mass, or go to Hell," meaning eternal salvation was assured only for people who attended Mass. The Gallup Poll of 1958 reported that 75 percent of Catholics attended Sunday Mass (D'Antonio et al. 1989, 44). The spiritual focus was strongly personal; sins were individual, such as lying, stealing, or expressing anger or sexuality (especially masturbating), and public questioning of the hierarchy unheard of (D'Antonio et al. 1996, 7–8). And just as sins were personal, so also was achieving salvation through confession and Communion, personal actions taken in accord with the Baltimore Catechism (the "rulebook" of the Church).

Millennial Catholics have grown up in a white-collar society, bene-fiting from all the gains their parents and grandparents made. Changes brought about by Vatican II have led them "to be more responsible for their faith journeys, more individualistic in their religious orientations and more inclined to think of themselves as spiritual but not religious. They are likely to do that for the rest of their lives" (D'Antonio et al. 2007, 149). And in this sense, they have indeed absorbed some of the Protestant ethos that continues to permeate American society, especially its suburbs.[2]

The two measures that revealed the greatest differences between the generations were found in (a) the strength of Catholic identity, in which one in three of the grandparents scored high in Catholic identity, while only 7 percent of the Millennials scored high; and (b) the level of commitment to the institutional Church, in which 43 percent of the grandparents' generation scored high, while no Millennials scored high.[3]

Millennial Catholics were a bit more likely than their grandparents to identify their Catholicism with their concern for the poor, with nine out of ten citing "Helping the Poor" as the most important Church teaching for them, which was also true for 84 percent of the grandparents (D'Antonio et al. 2007, 93). With other non-Catholic Millennials, they have shown strong support for environmental concerns and other social issues, suggesting that here they find resonance with the pope and Church leaders who speak out strongly for social justice (Carlin 2008, 1–15). Whether they will sustain this perspective on life in the face of the current economic climate with high joblessness rates remains to be seen.

To summarize briefly, research about American Catholics has found that, in the course of the past century, they have advanced from a position at the bottom of the education, occupation, and income ladder, during which time they also suffered significantly from prejudice and discrimination, to a position today where they are part of mainstream

---

[2] Michele Dillon and Paul Wink found that the American reliance on conscience over obedience goes back to the 1930s across all religious groups. See Dillon and Wink, *In the Course of a Lifetime: Tracing Religious Belief, Practice, and Change* (Berkeley: University of California Press, 2007).

[3] The three indicators used to create the Catholic Identity Index are (1) being Catholic is a very important part of who you are; (2) it is important that younger generations of your family grow up as Catholics; and (3) you can't imagine yourself being anything but Catholic. For details about the construction of the index and its results, see D'Antonio et al. 2007, 19–21. The three indicators used to construct the Commitment Index are (1) how important is the Catholic Church to you personally? (2) Mass attendance, and (3) would you ever consider leaving the Church? Full details about this index and its results are found in Ibid., 39–41.

America, where they have achieved many of the material goods available to the middle class and, by Church criteria, have fulfilled spiritual goals promised by the bishops who led the way in building the Catholic school system.

We turn now to examine the perceptions American Catholics have about the American Dream.

Polls: Perceptions of the American Dream

In this section, I rely on and compare a number of polls taken in the past decade that ask Americans about the American Dream. Although a majority of all Americans believe in the American Dream, the polls show some marked differences in the size of the majority as well as considerable variance in what the Dream is about. I begin with the polls of John Zogby. Zogby has been polling the American people for more than a decade about whether they believed in the American Dream, whether the Dream was more about material goods or spiritual goals, whether it was equally accessible to all Americans, and whether it may even have died. Zogby's findings (see Table 7.1) make clear that the great majority of Americans still believe in the Dream, with almost equal numbers saying it is more about material goods (38 percent) and 43 percent saying it is about finding spiritual happiness. American Catholics are very much like other Americans in these perceptions (40 and 41 percent, respectively).

Changes have developed over time. Table 7.1 shows that a decade ago (1998), twice as many Catholics thought that the Dream was mainly about finding spiritual happiness (52 percent) rather than material goods (23 percent). During the last decade, attitudes fluctuated gradually but steadily (Table 7.1), so that by 2009 Catholics were as likely to see the Dream as achieving material goods (40 percent) as spiritual happiness (41 percent)—a decline of eleven percentage points among those who now see it as seeking spiritual happiness, and a gain of seventeen percentage points among those saying material goals.

Although the percentages differ by religious group, all three show the same pattern of movement away from spiritual happiness toward material goods.

When poll respondents were asked directly if they, their families, or only their children could achieve the Dream, three in ten Catholics said they could achieve material success; another one in three said it was

TABLE 7.1 Importance of material goods and spiritual goals in achieving the American Dream, by religious affiliation

	Catholics (%)	Protestants (%)	Jews (%)
For you and your family, is the American Dream mainly about achieving material goods or is it more about finding spiritual happiness?			
1998			
a. Material goods	23	18	30
b. Spiritual happiness	52	61	50
2001			
a. Material goods	34	29	46
b. Spiritual happiness	49	54	34
2005			
a. Material goods	41	36	46
b. Spiritual happiness	42	49	34
2009 (January)			
a. Material goods	40	34	48
b. Spiritual happiness	41	48	24

Source: Zogby International polls about the American Dream, 1998–2009.

possible to achieve spiritual but not material success; 7 percent of Catholics said their children were more likely to attain the material success the Dream offers; and 14 percent said the Dream was beyond them, whether it was spiritual or material.[4]

When asked to choose the two factors that they believed most affected their ability to achieve this Dream, in both cases, almost six in ten said, (a) America is the land of opportunity, and (b) I am intelligent and work hard, so I should succeed. Eight percent said, "My religious faith ensures that I will find fulfillment."

On the other hand, when asked to explain the factors that best explained why they believed the American Dream does not exist for

---

[4] In a poll taken during the campaign in August 2008, 52 percent said the Dream was obtainable, while another 16 percent said they had obtained it. (Data not available controlling for religion.) About eight in ten said it was harder to achieve the Dream. (And when asked if they thought it would be easier or harder for the next generation to achieve the Dream, again, three out of four said it would be harder. And that was before the economic collapse of September 2008; Lake Research Partners, August 21, 2008).

them and their families, American Catholics said, (a) "The powers that be don't care about people like me" (43 percent), and (b) "Where I live it just costs too much, and . . . is just out of reach" (36 percent).

Unfortunately, these polls do not probe in depth why the tides have shifted. We can seek clues from the events between 1998 and 2009 that might shed light on changes in the way the Dream is perceived. A brief recession occurred in 2000–2001 after seven years of economic growth; terrorists attacked New York City's World Trade Center (the symbol of U.S. commercial power) and the Pentagon (the symbol of U.S. military power) on September 11, 2001; a sexual-abuse scandal rocked the Catholic Church; the Anglican Communion split over the consecration of an openly gay bishop; and increasing opposition to the war in Iraq coincided with the deteriorating situation in Afghanistan. We can only hypothesize about how these events have impacted Americans across generations.

Other polls during this time period cast a different light on Americans' perception of and feelings toward this Dream. For example, the Lake Poll (August 2008) included a set of questions that provided more specificity regarding what the Dream was or is than the broad terms "material" or "spiritual" goals that Zogby employed. It asked respondents to rank the importance to them of reaching a series of goals said to embody aspects of the American Dream. Table 7.2 provides the mean score on a scale of one to ten indicating the importance of seven items, with a mean score of 1 meaning "not important at all" and 10 meaning "an extremely important part of the American Dream."

All seven items received very strong support as being an extremely important part of the American Dream. But phrased as they were, none of the items suggests a purely material goal or achievement. If anything, they seem to include a mix of spiritual and material values and goals. It may be more accurate to say Americans see their goals as a blend of material and spiritual goods, beliefs, and values.

The CBS/*New York Times* survey of May 8, 2009, offers its own perspective on the Dream (Seelye 2009). The *Times* writer noted that, despite the deepness of the recession in 2009, the poll reported that "72% of Americans in this nationwide survey said they believed it is possible to start out poor in the United States, work hard and become rich, a classic definition of the American Dream" (Ibid.). It may help to understand the rags-to-riches dream when we know more about what Americans mean by "rich." In this survey, 51 percent said a family was

TABLE 7.2   Importance of individual components of the American Dream

	Mean score
Rate the importance of each item as part of the American Dream, using a scale from 0 to 10, where 10 means the item is extremely important, and 1 means it is not important at all.	
1. Being able to afford to own your own home	9.0
2. Being treated with respect for the work you do	9.0
3. Having affordable quality health care that you can depend on	9.2
4. Having a secure and dignified retirement	9.1
5. Being able to ensure your children have the opportunity to succeed	9.2
6. Having a job that pays enough to support a family	9.2
7. Owning your own small business	6.5

Source: Lake Poll, August 2008.

wealthy if its income fell between $100,000 and $400,000 per year; 16 percent categorized a family as wealthy with income between $400,000 and $1 million; 7 percent said the income was $1 million or more.

In reality, median household income in the year 2008 was $50,303 (in 2008 dollars), a decline of almost $2,000 from the 2007 level. According to a *New York Times* article on the 2000 census data, only 5.2 percent of all American wage earners earned salaries of $100,000 or more in the year 2000. That 72 percent believe it was possible to reach the $100,000 goal suggests the continuing strength of the Dream. But although they may have believed it was possible to go from rags to riches, their responses to other questions made clear that their own goals were much more modest.

When asked to explain exactly what the American Dream was:

27 percent said "freedom and opportunity"
18 percent said "being successful"
13 percent said "financial security and a job"
9 percent said "having a home"
6 percent said "happiness/peace of mind"

These responses provide more evidence that the Dream is a mix of values, beliefs, and achievements, material and spiritual and perhaps more in keeping with the respondents' real-life situations. This may help explain why the CBS/*New York Times* poll also reported that 44 percent said they had achieved the Dream, with another 31 percent saying they expected to within their lifetimes. Overall, comparing the three polls, the percentage of those who said they had already achieved it varied considerably (44 percent to 16 percent, with between 14 percent and 28 percent saying the Dream was beyond their ability to achieve). Although most Americans believe it is possible to go from rags to riches, their personal Dream goals are much more modest.

Social Order and the American Dream: The Government's Role, Real and Perceived

In the first section of this chapter, I examine research to help place Americans and Catholics in particular in generational context. In the second part, I examine a range of polls, some of which describe how Americans and Catholics, in particular, perceived the Dream in general and in their own lives. The polls examined above help us better understand how the American people see the American Dream and believe that they have achieved or may achieve it in their lifetimes.

In a June 2001 survey, Zogby asked about the importance of government in helping or hindering people from achieving the American Dream (see Table 7.3). Two out of three Catholics, Protestants, and Jews

TABLE 7.3 Beliefs regarding achievement of the American Dream, by religious affiliation

	Catholics (%)	Protestants (%)	Jews (%)
How significant has the government been in helping you achieve the American Dream?			
a. Very significant	9	8	16
b. Somewhat significant	22	25	18
c. Less than significant	24	21	16
d. Insignificant	43	42	51
e. Not sure	2	3	0
Is there equal opportunity for all Americans to achieve the American Dream?			
a. Yes	55	56	38
b. No	43	40	58
c. Not sure	2	4	4

Source: Zogby International polls about the American Dream, 1998–2009.

TABLE 7.4 Importance of government and political action in attainability of the American Dream

	Mean score
For each step that could be taken to help make the American Dream more attainable, use a scale from 0 to 10, where 10 means this step would be very effective, and 0 means the step would not be effective at all.	
1. Strong enforcement of the laws to prevent discrimination and ensure women and minorities get equal pay and have equal opportunity	8.1
2. Working people becoming politically active to hold politicians accountable	8.4
3. Government invests in job training and the green technologies that will be the engine of the economy in the twenty-first century	7.6
4. Government makes sure employers keep their promises to employees, including protecting their pensions and health care	8.6
5. Government guarantees that every American has access to quality, affordable health care	8.4

Source: Lake Poll, August 2008.

said the government was not very or at all significant in helping them achieve the American Dream. In fact, more Americans said the government's role was "Insignificant" than gave any other response.

Zogby also asked whether all Americans have equal opportunity to achieve the American Dream. The results are shown in Table 7.3. The phrase "equal opportunity" has been an important part of American political ideology from the beginning ("All men are created equal"), finding expression in legislation that provided women the right to vote (1920) and the Voting Rights Act of 1965, to cite just two examples.

I find further insights into the public's perception of the relationship between the Dream and the government's possible role in a question in the 2008 Lake Poll (see Table 7.4). Participants were asked to rate a series of steps that could be taken to help make the American Dream more attainable. The responses suggest that a great majority of Americans would look to the government to be an active supporter of their quests for the Dream. Missing is the question of whether they perceive the government to be able to carry out any of these desirable actions. Americans find themselves in the midst of a very slow recovery from the recession that began in December 2007 and continued through 2008–2009. The fact that two out of three Americans do not see the government's role to be a significant one in helping them achieve the Dream is probably an understatement in this environment.

The last seventy-five years have produced legislation that guaranteed at least a minimal amount of money every month to Americans who paid into Social Security or its government equivalent during their working lives. At present, "Social Security provides more than half the income for a majority of retirees" (Sloan 2010).

At the end of WWII, the government passed the GI Bill, providing educational and home-ownership opportunities for millions of World War II veterans and changing American society, creating a solid middle-class base that included just about all the white second- and third-generation ethnics; the government also passed legislation that made it possible for all Americans to deduct from their taxes the mortgage-interest payments on their homes.

The Voting Rights Act of 1965 made the 2008 election possible by finally ending the multiple ways that state and local governments had found to keep African Americans from exercising their rights to vote. Also in 1965, the government passed Medicare legislation, which is now available to senior citizens. Medicaid is available for poor families, and Pell grants help more young people achieve college educations.

Social Security, Medicare, and Medicaid have made it possible for millions of senior citizens to live fairly safe and secure lives, enabling their children and grandchildren to be free of the financial responsibility of caring for them even as they struggle to get through their own family growth periods. Given that as many as 41 percent of Americans have said they have achieved the Dream, the fact that two-thirds did not see the role of government as significant in the quest for the Dream suggests that distrust of the government, seen in so many polls in the past decades, runs deep. A negative perception of government definitely exists, perhaps having its current stimulus originating with Ronald Reagan's statement that "the government is the problem." As the sociological dictum states, "If things are perceived to be real, they are real in their consequences." And the consequences are that the American people have had a long-standing distrust of the government, such that even though they can check off a list of things they would like to see the government do, they fail to recognize the role the government plays in helping them achieve the Dream.

Is the strong sense of individual achievement such that we have made it difficult to understand and to appreciate the nature of the social order of things, from conception through the family care most of us still enjoy into our adulthood to the social support provided by governments local and national?

Social Class and the American Dream

A second way in which the Dream is challenged relates directly to the economy and the belief that anyone can rise from poverty to become rich.

Even as we continue to sing our praises to the Dream, research scholars are hard at work trying to test measures that can be said to be indicators of Dream achievement.

Under the heading "The 'American Dream': Still a Reality?" John Macionis summarized years of research on social mobility, reporting that around 1970, the upward trend slowed to a halt, "ushering in a period of income stagnation that has shaken our national confidence" (Macionis 1999). People were working more hours just to maintain their income levels; the percentage of low-income earners rose from 12 to 15 percent; and "fully 50 percent of young people, aged eighteen to twenty-four, are now living with their parents" (Ibid., 274). Ten years later, the research findings were just as bleak.

Eugene Robinson, in a *Washington Post* feature story, examined the findings from the Economic Mobility Project, a research initiative carried out by the Pew Charitable Trusts, which, among other things, compared the income of parents of the 1960s with that of their children in the late 1990s and early 2000s (Robinson 2007). Among the key findings:

1. Less upward mobility (that is, from bottom to top) exists in the United States (only 6 percent) than in Great Britain (which is thought to have a more sharply defined class structure).
2. Although Americans move "fairly easily up and down the middle rungs of the ladder, there is 'stickiness' at the ends."
3. Four out of ten children who are born poor will remain poor.
4. "The personal income of American men—including white men—has been almost perfectly flat for the past three decades."

John Morton, Pew's managing editor, stated it simply: "Traditionally, Americans have been ready to accept high levels of inequality because of our belief in the American dream. What happens if we can't believe in the dream any longer?" (Ibid.). I ask, when will Americans come to realize the importance of the economic structures in aiding or restraining their quests?

Catholic Teachings on Social Justice and the American Dream

Beginning in the latter part of the nineteenth century, with the writings of Pope Leo XIII, Catholic Church leaders (clergy and laity) developed what are commonly called the "Catholic social teachings," a new concern for the common good. Mainline Protestants began to develop their own "social gospel teachings" in the early part of the twentieth century. Jews with their history of close communal ties have long held views about having a responsibility to contribute to the common well-being. In this last section, I focus on the Catholic social teachings, how they developed, and questions about their future in the hands of the Millennial Generation.

During the course of the twentieth century, Catholic Church teachings evolved from a focus on personal salvation built around confessing one's sins regularly, repentance and reconciliation, and then communion with obedience to a complex and extended set of rules that guaranteed salvation. By the time of Franklin Roosevelt's New Deal, Catholic social teachings fit well with much of the New Deal program. Vatican Council II (1962–1965) provided even more stimulus for change that acknowledged freedom of conscience, personal responsibility, and an openness to the larger world within which the Church was seen now as a co-worker for the common good. Many Catholics believe the government has a moral responsibility to act at all levels, including the national, to see that the needs of the people will be met. Moderate and conservative Catholics believe that "subsidiarity"—acting at the lowest level that will do the job effectively—is the only way that one has a responsibility to act. For many conservative Catholics, this means personal piety toward the poor and needy. They oppose government intervention at the national level, because they argue that such efforts are wasted on building bureaucracies.

Two articles in the March 2009 issue of *U.S. Catholic* (a monthly magazine) reveal the challenge to this nation to make Catholic social justice teachings come alive in a capitalist economy in a time of crisis. "American Dreams Deferred," by Matt Bigelow and Megan Sweas, focuses on the efforts of the U.S. Conference of Catholic Bishops to "create . . . affordable housing so that families can have a safe decent place to live that's in a community" (Bigelow and Sweas 2009, 16). Its efforts have included support for a bill creating a National Housing Trust Fund. The bill, passed in 2008, should have become available in 2010 but awaits funding for the construction and restoration of low-income housing (Ibid.). Still, the authors admit, long-term support for such bills to help the poor is thin indeed. In a collapsing economy, it becomes even thinner.

"Can This Market Be Saved?" by Daniel Finn, professor of Theology and Economics at St. John's University in Collegeville, Minnesota, raises even more challenges as he spells out the implications of the Catholic ethic of social justice in a rapidly globalizing, urbanizing world that is in economic free fall. He asserts that the Catholic ethic of the common good seeks the attainment of the good life by all. This good life includes schools, museums, parks, police forces, peace, and so forth, which "we all depend on but that no one person generates" (Finn 2009, 13). Everyone should have access to a minimum quality of life: "Nobody can be left out." In the view of this Catholic ethic, markets should not be designed only to enable individuals to maximize their own personal well-being; Catholic ethic requires also "actions and policies that benefit the poor and all who need assistance" (Ibid., 14). Finn emphasizes the point this way: "It was wrong for last year's [2008] government stimulus checks to go to taxpayers but not to those too poor to pay taxes. Not only are the poor worthy of our help, but they spend all their income and would have spent all their stimulus check. Most folks saved some of the check, so it stimulated the economy less than if the poor had gotten the money" (Ibid.).

Finn explains how a moral economy includes the commitment to a just wage—that is, one that provides a sufficient income to support a family of four with adequate food, health care, education, and housing. To the extent that this ethic may be said to ground a Catholic version of the American Dream, we can say that many of the bills adopted during the New Deal, including Social Security, low-cost housing mortgages, deduction of mortgage-interest payments from taxes, the GI Bill, the expansion of higher education, and Medicaid and Medicare, would all qualify as aspects of such an ethic. Indeed, at the time of the current economic crisis, about two-thirds of all U.S. citizens possessed home-owner mortgages.

Is this Catholic ethic for the common good relevant in a time of economic crisis? Is this not a Catholic version of what the historian Adams meant by a social order that enables everyone to achieve their maximum potential? Is the younger generation of Catholics able to look beyond its own threatened well-being to the needs of the common in the face of so much uncertainty? The building of the Catholic school system was a communal experience, the building of a social order within the order of the larger society, with thousands of religious women who devoted their lives with little or no financial recompense, and millions of Catholics whose financial giving was often made not from their surplus but from their substance.

In a time of extraordinary economic and social distress that threatens our personal and social well-being, Obama's election was seen by many as an opportunity to shift our thinking away from the more material elements in the American Dream (new house, car, clothes) to the more spiritual or simply nonmaterial, such as a cleaner environment, health care for all, a turn away from militarism, and so forth. Are Americans ready for such a change in direction, one that would have us more concerned about doing things that would improve the air we breathe, the way we use our resources, and other actions that would foster the common good? As of this writing, with the unemployment rate hovering around 10 percent, the Obama administration has had to juggle its lofty goals of changing our environment to make it significantly healthier, with the felt need to create jobs and to stimulate buying material goods, such as automobiles and houses. This situation explains, for example, the continuing struggle that allows mountaintop coal mining in West Virginia rather than an action that would increase unemployment.

In 1884, the U.S. Catholic bishops met in Baltimore and formally committed the Church to building the parochial school system that became the heart and soul of the great Catholic parishes that dominated so much of Catholic urban life through the 1950s. That achievement seems to me the example par excellence of the American Dream writ large. The bishops found a way to bridge the quest for material goods with the search for spiritual happiness and the salvation of souls. Research findings from studies of such groups as VOTF, Call to Action, and Intentional Eucharistic Communities all show high levels of Catholic school education. They are also among the leaders in promoting the Catholic social teachings.

A new study (Gray and Cidade 2010) provides comparisons between Catholics attending Catholic colleges and universities and Catholics attending other colleges and universities on a range of questions dealing with Catholic beliefs, attitudes, and practices. The sample is one of Catholics between the ages of eighteen and twenty-four (Millennials). Several of the findings provide evidence of their high commitment to the ethic of the common good, which may in turn affect how the Dream is perceived and lived in their time. For example, "Catholic students in Catholic colleges are more likely than Catholics at other colleges to move toward the Church's teachings on general statements of social justice." Fifty-eight percent of Catholics who are juniors at Catholic colleges agreed "either somewhat or strongly that the wealthy should pay higher taxes. And an even higher percentage of Catholics at other colleges and universities agree with this Catholic Church policy" (Ibid., 13).

Discussion and Conclusion

When I was growing up, my attention was focused on my personal conduct, with little or no attention to a larger social ethic, much less any understanding of the Church's emerging social teachings. As I began to read about them in my twenties and thirties, I came to recognize how they were realized in varying degrees in the legislation of the New Deal. In an important sense, Catholic support for the Democratic Party was support for social legislation that reflected Catholic social teachings. The Reagan era in U.S. politics turned us inward with its focus on individual entrepreneurship encapsulated by Reagan's famous aphorism, "the government is the problem." To which Paul Volcker, once again a voice in the midst of the 2009 crisis, replied so trenchantly in 1990, "If you think the government is the problem, then there are no solutions."[5]

The well-established linkage between education, occupation, and income makes it clear that achieving the Dream is complex, multifaceted, and highly relative, a crucial point if we are to make sense of it in our history. Research has made clear that one of the things that makes the Dream seem so within reach in the United States is the generally held belief that ours is a more or less classless society. And this belief is grounded in the *Horatio Alger* and a thousand other stories purporting to show that, in the United States, anyone can rise from rags to riches. Thus, the reality that there are very real and, in the past thirty years, increasing gaps in income levels is obscured by the belief that we can leapfrog from one level to another if we just work hard enough.

The Dream in this sense is promoted as a highly personal goal, yet one that we could and should all strive to achieve. We like to believe it is we as individuals who achieved good or poor grades in school,

---

[5] Statement made on occasion of Dr. Volcker's receiving the Common Wealth Award in Wilmington, Delaware, March 1990. I was present on that occasion.

depending on the level of our aspirations and willingness to work. We assert that we achieve as individuals (my college education). But during the 1940s and 1950s, that reality clashed with the growing reality of school segregation, denial of voting rights, and unequal employment opportunities. Whether it was recognized as such at the time, the Voting Rights Act of 1965 was a key mechanism fostered by the federal government that helped make reality of Obama's dream. Thus, we glimpse the response to the question, "What role does playing by a set of rules have in fostering and sustaining the American Dream?" To me, in the sixth grade, the poem was telling me that I, too, could become president, if I "no tella no lies" and "worka hard." For students who went to schools, parochial or public, and who played by the rules, the Dream manifested itself in a variety of ways. And for African Americans who had been living in this country longer than some white Europeans, the Voting Rights Act provided the rules by which they finally achieved a share of political power.

During the course of my lifetime, I have been the beneficiary of what I take to be Zogby's two distinct aspects of the American Dream: spiritual and material well-being. I have lived through the Depression and World War II and benefited from an extraordinary education (made possible by scholarships provided by people of a different generation and time, and in part by the G.I. Bill, made possible by American taxpayers). I have benefited from the pleasure of home ownership and discretionary income.

I have written about the values and beliefs that ground our pluralistic democracy and participated in many of the events of Vatican II, a dream that became a reality for millions of Catholics around the world and that now has its own problems with its own crisis.

I have seen the poem I recited in 1937 apparently realized in the election of Obama in 2008. I have seen my appreciation for the Catholic Church's social teachings grow, and I have seen my own research reveal a new Millennial Generation of young people (including our own children and grandchildren) embracing the meaning of the Church's teachings on social justice even as the crisis deepens. I close with the realization that the American people continue to see the Dream as a personal achievement and continue to see the government as failing to meet their needs and wants, even as their own actions in electing people who oppose what they call "big government" leads to weakening the very government from which they want more—at no extra cost.

Factors seen as essential to the realization of the American Dream include freedom of opportunity, equal access to the important institutions of society, and playing by the rules. In all three cases, it is belief in freedom of opportunity, equal access, and playing by the rules more than the actual degree to which these factors are available to the great mass of citizens that helps keep the dream alive. More problematic is how ethno-racial-religious factors have in the past, continue in the present, and may continue in the future to define what the Dream is or to make it easier or more difficult to have freedom of opportunity, equal access, and knowledge of the rules that enable us to achieve the Dream.

Ultimately, I find that the Dream as it now exists in the minds of Americans reveals a huge gap in this society between how we see ourselves as individuals and how we understand our relationships with the social institutions of our society. Do young adults concern themselves about maintaining their holds on the Dream? Is their Dream different or less well defined? Is that difference due in part at least to their awareness of living in a different world, a world larger than the borders of the United States?

They are discovering this world via the Internet, the iPod, blogging, and whatever else modern technology enables. If the Dream has a universal quality—that is, if the Dream transcends any particular religious or other racial-ethnic, regional, or national ideology—do the facts of American life across generations continue to give substance to the Dream? Or do the facts of American life today lead us inexorably toward a new world perspective on the Dream? The 2008 national elections seemed to be a kind of apotheosis of the American Dream perceived worldwide.

Question: Now that the white European ex-ethnics have made it, are they more likely to step on the hands of those trying to climb the ladder or to reach down and help them? Is there any basis for even imagining the latter? The Millennials have much more education and technology at their disposal and a measured sense of concern for the common good. They may well support higher taxes for the wealthy as a way to help pay for common good programs. Will the Millennials help forge a social order that focuses less on rags to riches and more on the values derived from a mix of the Catholic, Protestant, Jewish, Muslim, and other progressive visions of the good society that the phrase "the common good" encompasses?

References

Adams, J. T. 1931. *The epic of America.* Bethesda, MD: Simon.

Bigelow, M., and M. Sweas. 2009. American dreams deferred. *U.S. Catholic,* March.

Carlin, C. 2008. *The young vote: Engaging America's youth in the 2008 elections and beyond.* Washington, DC: Brookings Institution.

D'Antonio, W. V., J. D. Davidson, D. R. Hoge, and M. L. Gautier. 2007. *American Catholics today: New realities of their faith and their church.* Lanham, MD: Rowman and Littlefield.

D'Antonio, W. V., J. D. Davidson, D. Hoge, and R. Wallace. 1989. *American Catholic laity in a changing church.* Kansas City, MO: Sheed and Ward.

———. 1996. *Laity, American and Catholic: Transforming the church.* Kansas City, MO: Sheed and Ward.

D'Antonio, W. V., and D. R. Hoge. 2006. The American experience of religious disestablishment and pluralism. *Social Compass* 53, no. 3: 345–356.

D'Antonio, W., and A. Pogorelc. 2007. *Voices of the faithful: Loyal Catholics striving for change.* New York: Crossroad.

Finn, D. 2009. Can this market be saved? *U.S. Catholic,* March.

Fiorenza, Bishop J. A. 1999. Presidential address, U.S. Conference of Catholic Bishops, Washington, DC, November 15.

Froehle, B. T., and M. L. Gautier. 2000. *Catholicism USA: A portrait of the Catholic Church in the United States.* Maryknoll, NY: Orbis Books.

Gray, M., and M. Cidade. 2010. *Catholicism on campus: Stability and change in Catholic student faith by college type.* Washington, DC: Center for Applied Research in the Apostolate, Georgetown University.

Gray, M., and M. Gautier. 2006. *A Special Report on U.S. Catholic Elementary Schools* 2000–2005. National Catholic Educational Association.

Lake Research Partners. 2008. *American dream survey, CTW presidential convention poll.* August 21.

Macionis, J. J. 1999. *Sociology: Annotated instructor's edition.* Saddle River, NJ: Prentice Hall.

Robinson, E. 2007. Tattered dream: Who'll tackle the issue of upward mobility? *Washington Post,* November 23.

Seelye, K. O. 2009. What happens to the American dream in a recession? *NewYorkTimes.com,* May 8. Available at www.nytimes.com/2009/05/08/us/08dreampoll.html?_&sqr=1.

Sloan, A. 2010. Social security could be the next to need a bailout. *Washington Post,* February 2.

Zogby International. *Polls on American Dream by Zogby International.*

CONCLUSION

 # The American Dream

Where Are We?

Sandra L. Hanson
John Kenneth White

THE AMERICAN DREAM has been a dominant theme in U.S. culture from the very beginning. But these are difficult times for Dreamers. Large numbers of Americans are unemployed, living in poverty, and without health care insurance. Jim Cullen (2003) and others (Ho 2007; Johnson 2006; Moen and Roehling 2005; Shapiro 2004) have suggested that the American Dream and this "glue" that binds us together may be unraveling, as we see a growing wealth gap, ongoing race inequality, an expanding poor immigrant population, and continued sexism in all aspects of American life. Perhaps the twenty-first century is not a time of increasing progress toward the American Dream. And middle-class Americans are not being spared. Downsizing and restructuring are here to stay as jobs go to cheaper markets. The growing distress across socioeconomic groups is a trend that began before the recent economic downturn and will most likely continue (Ehrenreich 2005). Public-opinion polls show that most Americans think that hard work alone affects one's ability to achieve the American Dream—suggesting that those who do not get ahead are somehow at fault (Hanson and Zogby forthcoming). Some have speculated that America has lost its way as well as its legacy of core values of economic and social justice (Kochan 2005). Is the American Dream so much a part of the fabric of American society that we fail to question it—regardless of whether we have full access to it (Johnson 2006)?

Our goal was to examine how the American Dream is doing in the twenty-first century given these historic social and economic conditions.

The authors discuss the history of the American Dream and its enduring significance in American life. They discuss the complexity of the Dream and its intersection with politics, religion, race, gender, and generation. The conclusions that the authors draw provide optimism about the faith that most Americans have regarding the possibility of achieving the American Dream as well as a realistic assessment of the cracks in the Dream that exist for women and minorities but also an increasing number of Americans across race, gender, and social-class groups. The authors provide evidence of a new hope for the Dream with the election of President Barack Obama. They also provide warnings on the need for better programs and policies that would make the Dream a reality for a larger number of Americans. What are the key conclusions and recommendations regarding the American Dream in the twenty-first century from the point of view provided by an interdisciplinary group of scholars? And what are these scholars' thoughts on the influence that President Obama has had on the American Dream?

Cullen (Chapter 1) suggests that the first decade of the twenty-first century has not been a particularly good one in American life. He argues that imperial overstretch in Iraq, indebtedness at home and abroad, and political corruption in the electoral process have created anxieties that our system of government and way of life may be breaking down. It is widely believed that the American Dream is the product of a historically unique exceptionalism, which is rooted in a particular location and political structure codified in the Declaration of Independence. In fact, Cullen argues that many of the most cherished aspects of the American Dream, such as upward mobility, have clear antecedents in other civilizations. Moreover, the American Dream as it developed preceded the creation of the United States and has survived its transformation from a de jure republic to a de facto empire under the current leadership of Obama, whose political appeal is in no small measure a perception of the degree to which he embodies the American Dream. Cullen concludes that, culturally democratic, the Dream is likely to survive the demise of that empire and suggests that it is worth considering what our lives would be like without it as a means of understanding where we currently stand.

Michael Kimmage considers the politics of the American Dream over the past few decades in Chapter 2. His chapter begins with a distinction regarding the American Dream. There is the material reality of the American Dream, the actual state of the economy, and the actual prospect for social advancements. Then there is the Dream itself, the hope that one will advance. Kimmage then applies this distinction to twentieth-century political history, starting with Franklin Roosevelt and ending with Obama. The finding is that successful American presidents have a clear language for articulating the American Dream and one that is related to their historical moment: FDR made a sober, moderate appeal to the American Dream during the Great Depression; Ronald Reagan used the American Dream to convey a national self-confidence. Success and failure follow cycles in party politics. Jimmy Carter's inability to reference the American Dream coincided with the larger decline of the Democratic Party in the 1970s. George W. Bush's relationship to the American Dream was overshadowed by his war against terror and then by the economic crisis, with a subsequent decline in the fortunes of the Republican Party. The American Dream's enduring stature in American politics, Kimmage argues, is visible in Obama's frequent references to Martin Luther King's dream and in the title of Obama's first autobiography, *Dreams from My Father*.

John White expands on the background and history of the American Dream in Chapter 3 by noting how the American Dream and the U.S. presidency are inextricably intertwined. He argues that nearly from its inception, American presidents have used the up-from-the-bootstraps-to-success stories that are embodied in the concept of the American Dream to make vital connections to voters. In many ways, White notes that presidents are the chief priests in the American civil religion, since one requirement of the job is to continuously express their faith in the American Dream and the possibilities for its renewal. Obama is the latest president to understand the power of the American Dream, and he used it to sell himself to the American people at a propitious moment in history when Americans sought to have the American Dream revitalized. White's chapter reveals how Obama's personal story, from his humble beginnings in Hawaii, born to parents without means, to his childhood in Indonesia and his success in climbing the educational and political ladders to extraordinary success in becoming the first African American president, is not just a compelling story but one that contains an important lesson to all Americans regardless of race: You, too, can make it. White concludes that, in telling his tale, Obama established an important link to his constituents and enhanced his powers as president.

James Loewen looks at race and the American Dream in Chapter 4. He concludes that American Dreams of a "good life" are racially tinged.

In part, this happens because we dream about what we know, and what we know in the United States is residential segregation by race. Loewen's chapter provides a background on racial segregation in the United States. He argues that our society was not always so segregated. Until around 1890, Americans lived much more integrated lives, racially and economically. Between 1890 and 1940, however, racism rose to new heights, and race relations sank to new depths, prompting historians to call this era the "nadir of race relations." Loewen provides detail on how this racism became embedded in our geography. The separation took a toll on African American morale and made it more likely that African Americans would receive inferior educations, health care, and other public services. Loewen details the implications for African Americans and their American Dreams. He concludes that to change our American Dream, we must change our racial geography. What do we do? Loewen recommends that every sundown town and county in the nation needs to take three steps: Admit it, apologize, and reform. He advises that, until a proven sundown town or county takes these steps, the United States (and states) should disallow the mortgage-interest exemption from their residents' income-tax filings. The election of America's first black president in 2008 was a step toward a more integrated nation, and Americans saw it that way. But Loewen argues that the transformation is hardly complete. Obama won the presidency with just over 40 percent of the votes of white males and only 10 percent of those in the Deep South; despite his win, racism is not an aberration in our society but a central part of it. As African American families try to pursue the American Dream, they still face special obstacles. During the summer of 2009, it became clear that the subprime mortgage loan crisis hit African Americans especially hard. Thus the American Dreams of many families—especially black families—turned to nightmares.

In Chapter 5, Sandra Hanson notes the long history of the American Dream and the assumption that the Dream is for all. The potential divide in the Dream that she considers is the gender divide. Hanson superimposes data on gender equality in areas involving education, occupations, income, and politics with public-opinion data showing how men and women feel about the American Dream. Her findings reveal progress yet considerable inequality by gender in many areas of American life associated with the Dream. Today, women attend college and graduate from college at a higher rate than men, but they continue to enter majors that assure them of occupations in lower-status, lower-paid, female-dominated occupations. Working women average seventy-seven cents to a man's dollar. Hanson finds that men and women are much more similar in their attitudes about the American Dream than in their achievement of it. In spite of this shared optimism, Hanson's data does reveal some differences in how men and women view the Dream and its possibility. She finds that women are more likely than men to think of the Dream in spiritual terms (rather than economic), and they are more likely to acknowledge inequality in the ability to achieve the American Dream. In her analysis of public-opinion items before and after President Obama's election, Hanson finds that women (but not men) became more optimistic about the chances of their children having a better life than them. With regard to the remaining gender gap in educational and occupational indicators of the American Dream, Hanson provides a number of policy recommendations. These include, for example, allowing flexible careers and occupational paths that acknowledge family obligations; promoting families in our economic and legislative policies and practices, not just wealth accumulation; and enforcing laws, such as Title VII, Title IX, and the Equal Pay Act, that prohibit gender inequality and sexual harassment.

John Zogby uses data from his public-opinion polls to examine attitudes about the American Dream over the past few decades in Chapter 6. He addresses questions about how Americans define the American Dream and whether they think it is achievable. He looks at these issues across generations of Americans. Zogby conceptualizes a model of American Dreamers that distinguishes between different versions of the Dream. His examination of post–September 11 polls suggests a dramatic shift in the nature of the American Dream, with a move away from a material definition and toward a more spiritual definition. Additionally, data are provided that reveal distinct attitudes among America's youth (he calls them the "First Global" generation) who are connected to the rest of the world like no other generation. This generation and their new view on the world have partially contributed to the move away from a materialistic version of the American Dream. Zogby notes that the "Dreamless Dead"—those who do not believe in the American Dream—was one of President Obama's largest support groups during the campaign. He notes that Americans remain optimistic about the Dream, but it is a time of great social and economic anxiety. Zogby's conclusions focus on the implications of these shifts for changes in the nature of American character. He suggests that Americans (and their

American Dreams) must face a new reality where excess is no longer possible. This, he concludes, is where President Obama has the skills to lead—toward a government that is fair and provides opportunity for all.

The final chapter (Chapter 7) in the volume is a Catholic reflection that considers the American Dream in the context of religion and generations. Bill D'Antonio explores the meaning and experience of the American Dream as it was perceived and lived out during the twentieth century for those Tom Brokaw has called the "Greatest Generation" and as it is currently perceived and experienced by those D'Antonio calls the Millennial Generation. Within that context, D'Antonio reflects on how the Roman Catholic Church in the United States might have impacted the lives of American Catholics in their quest for the American Dream. The comparison of the grandparents with the grandchildren allows one to examine the American Dream as it has been lived throughout a period of a full century. D'Antonio's look at Catholicism makes a distinction between a Dream that focuses on the individual and one that focuses on the community. He discusses the building of the Catholic school system as a communal experience. D'Antonio notes the irony in the fact that Catholics in the suburbs today with higher incomes and more discretionary funds than their forbearers have been less willing to pay the price to build the Catholic schools for the twenty-first century. And so the question arises as to whether they may have become more self-centered than community-centered in their perspectives about the Dream as they go about living the middle-class suburban way. D'Antonio ends his chapter with this question: Will the Millennials help forge a social order that focuses less on rags to riches and more on the values derived from a mix of religious and other progressive visions of the good society that the phrase "the common good" encompasses?

These are historic times. Americans are being hit with a great recession like no other. Rates of unemployment, underemployment, poverty, and homelessness are at unprecedented levels. Given this, have Americans stopped dreaming? The experts in this volume provide considerable insight into the answer to this question, and their research suggests that the answer is a qualified "no"—Americans have not stopped dreaming. A March 2010 public-opinion poll by Zogby shows that although the percentage of Americans who believe that it is possible for them and their families to achieve the American Dream is down, a majority of Americans (57 percent) still believe. But evidence *does* show that the nature of the Dream is shifting. Chapters by Hanson, Zogby, and

D'Antonio show a shift toward a more spiritual (and less materialist) version of the Dream. The shift began after September 11 and continues during the economic recession. The spiritual component of the Dream is especially large among the young generation, which Zogby refers to as the First Global Generation and D'Antonio refers to as the Millennial Generation. D'Antonio's chapter notes the necessity for a continued shift toward a more communal and less individualistic version of the Dream.

Part of the answer as to why this Dream persists comes from the chapters by Cullen, White, and Kimmage that consider the history of the American Dream. Cullen argues that the Dream of upward mobility is an old Dream that has antecedents in earlier civilizations. It is, however, the basis of American exceptionalism, and almost every U.S. president has embodied it as a way to connect to American voters. White and Kimmage argue that President Obama, the first elected African American U.S. president, has embodied this Dream more than any other. Public-opinion polls examined in chapters by Hanson, Zogby, and D'Antonio show the importance of this president for the Dream during these difficult economic times. Given the connection between presidents and Dreams that White and Kimmage develop, it is impossible to predict how alive the Dream would be under a different president whose life was not so clearly a personal embodiment of the American Dream.

Our conclusions note that the authors provide a qualified "no" to the question of whether the American Dream is dead. The nature of the qualification is developed in the chapters by Loewen and Hanson, which look at the race and gender divides in the American Dream. These authors provide a cautionary note in thinking about a Dream that involves equal access for all. Loewen focuses on racial segregation and the central role that racism still plays in U.S. society in spite of the step toward integration that occurred with President Obama's election. Hanson's chapter examines a continued gender divide in education, occupations, income, and politics. In spite of the gender gap in achievement, she shows that a majority of women *do* believe in the American Dream. Although public-opinion polls reveal they are less optimistic than men, they have become more optimistic about the Dream with the election of President Obama. It is optimism, layered with the reality of difficult economic times, that leads the authors of this volume to argue for the continued presence of an American Dream. The Dream has survived difficult periods. It stayed alive during times when women and blacks could not vote and during the economic crisis of the Great Depression. The authors suggest that shifts in how we define the Dream are taking place, and part of their optimism comes from a new version of the Dream that is more focused on equity, equality, and community rather than material success and economic mobility.

References

Cullen, J. 2003. *The American Dream: A short history of an idea that shaped a nation.* New York: Oxford University Press.

Ehrenreich, B. 2005. *Bait and switch: The (futile) pursuit of the American Dream.* New York: Henry Holt.

Hanson, S. L., and J. Zogby. Forthcoming. The polls—trends: Attitudes about the American Dream. *Public Opinion Quarterly* (forthcoming).

Ho, A. K. 2007. *Achieving the American Dream.* Lanham, MD: Hamilton Books.

Johnson, H. B. 2006. *The American Dream and the power of wealth: Choosing schools and inheriting wealth in the land of opportunity.* New York: Routledge.

Kochan, T. A. 2005. *Restoring the American Dream.* Cambridge, MA: MIT Press.

Moen, P., and P. Roehling. 2005. *The career mystique: Cracks in the American Dream.* Lanham, MD: Rowman and Littlefield.

Shapiro, T. M. 2004. *The hidden cost of being African American: How wealth perpetuates inequality.* New York: Oxford University Press.

 # Contributors

Jim Cullen teaches history at the Ethical Culture Fieldston School in New York. He is the author of many books, among them *Born in the USA: Bruce Springsteen and the American Tradition* (1997, 2005) and *The American Dream: A Short History of an Idea that Shaped a Nation* (2003). He is also a book review editor for the History News Network.

William V. D'Antonio is a fellow of the Institute for Policy Research and Catholic Studies, The Catholic University of America. His fourteen books cover religion and politics, including most recently *American Catholics Today: New Realities of Their Faith and Their Church* (2007).

Sandra L. Hanson is a professor of sociology at The Catholic University of America. She is the author of several books on gender, race, and science. Her latest is *Swimming Against the Tide: African American Girls in Science Education* (2009).

Michael C. Kimmage is an associate professor of history at The Catholic University of America. His first book is *The Conservative Turn: Lionel Trilling, Whittaker Chambers, and the Lessons of Anti-Communism* (2009).

James W. Loewen taught race relations for twenty years at the University of Vermont. He is the author of a number of award-winning books on race in America, including *Sundown Towns: A Hidden Dimension of American Racism* (2005) and *Lies My Teacher Told Me: Everything Your*

American History Textbook Got Wrong (1995). His most recent books are *Teaching What Really Happened: How to Avoid the Tyranny of Textbooks and Get Students Excited about Doing History* (2009) and *The Confederate and Neo-Confederate Reader: The "Great Truth" about the "Lost Cause"* (2010; co-edited with Edward H. Sebesta). He now lives in Washington, D.C., continuing his research on how Americans remember their past.

John Kenneth White is a professor of politics at The Catholic University of America. He is the author of several books on political parties and the American presidency. His latest is *Barack Obama's America: How New Conceptions of Race, Family, and Religion Ended the Reagan Era* (2009).

John Zogby is a pollster and chairman of IBOPE–Zogby International. He has polled in over eighty countries and on behalf of governments, nongovernmental agencies, the world's largest brand companies, and prominent news media. He is the author of the critically acclaimed *The Way We'll Be: The Zogby Report on the Transformation of the American Dream* (2008). He writes weekly columns for Forbes.com and *US News and World Report,* as well as a monthly column for *Politics.*

Index